Successful
Cold Call
Selling

Successful Cold Call Selling

Lee Boyan

amacom

American Management Association

This book is available at a special discount when ordered in bulk quantities. For information, contact Special Sales Department, AMACOM, a division of American Management Association, 135 West 50th Street, New York, NY 10020.

Library of Congress Cataloging in Publication Data

Boyan, Lee.
  Successful cold call selling.

  Includes bibliographical references and index.
  1. Selling. 2. Direct selling. 3. Telephone selling. I. Title.
HF5438.25.B68   1983   658.8'5   83-45211
ISBN 0-8144-5771-1
ISBN 0-8144-7639-2

First AMACOM paperback edition 1985.

Printing number

10   9   8   7   6   5   4   3   2

What This Book Will Do For You

You are about to learn powerful, proven techniques that will enable you to perform at your best whenever you introduce yourself to a new prospect either in person or by phone. You will master the ability to gain an audience that has top-level buying authority as you arrange to present your offering under the most favorable circumstances, and you will come out with orders where no business had previously existed.

To be able to do this self-assuredly and consistently is heady wine indeed. There is and always will be insatiable demand for persons with such skill.

My 30 years of experience as a salesperson, field sales trainer, seminar leader, professional speaker, and management consultant have provided me with countless opportunities to meet thousands of sales executives from all kinds of businesses. My association with them was often more than a casual acquaintance. Many times we worked closely together, planning sales campaigns, sales meetings, and training programs, and developing new concepts to use in my sales and management seminars.

I have learned a great deal from my association with these

executives. If I had to single out the one skill they value most of all in their men and women, it would be the ability to create new business, instead of just being order takers.

Taking orders for something buyers are ready and waiting to buy at a price they are willing to pay can usually be done by salespeople with average ability. But the highest rewards, both financial and intangible, go to those who are able to create new business through their ingenious efforts.

> Do you ever feel uneasy when you make an introductory call to a new prospect either by phone or in person?
>
> Do you vastly prefer to call on repeat customers or familiar prospects rather than strangers?
>
> Do you feel that making "cold calls" is unproductive?
>
> Do you ever get thrown off balance by a harsh rebuff?
>
> When an appointment is canceled or a call is finished sooner than expected, do you often find yourself without fill-in prospects to call on?
>
> Do you often have difficulty getting past a receptionist or a secretary?
>
> Do you often have to settle for making presentations to persons who are not top buying authority?
>
> Do you ever find yourself at a loss for words when a prospect resists granting you an interview?
>
> Do you ever wish you could have a second chance to make a particular first impression?
>
> Do you often find it difficult to gain the attention of prospects who are preoccupied with other important matters?
>
> Do you have an effective strategy for dealing with these situations?

If you answered yes to any question except the last one, you will find specific ideas in this book that will vastly increase your selling power.

If you answered no to the last question, this book will build a selling strategy that will change your selling career for the better, once and for all.

I have seen dramatic positive changes in the performance of

many salespeople, some who doubled and tripled their sales production after learning just a few of the techniques set forth in this book. In some cases they were shy even to the point of being called introverted. Yet today they are enjoying high incomes plus a newly found self-confidence by creatively selling big-ticket products and services to top-level executives.

When you master the techniques revealed in this book, you too will gain a great deal of personal and economic security. You will never be out of a job. You can, on your own initiative, increase your income anytime you want. You will also have a most rewarding feeling of poise and a sense of control over the direction of your life—poise not only in the business world of selling, but also in the entire range of interpersonal relationships.

It is important to read and understand each chapter in proper sequence. In later chapters you will be given specific techniques and explicit words and phrases to use at the point of introduction to a strange prospect that are sure to open new doors for you. But the words and phrases will ring true and the techniques will work their magic only if you fully understand and adhere to the principles that unfold in the earlier chapters. Although some of these principles extend to all phases of selling, this book primarily concerns their all-important impact during the opening move.

Now let's begin your first step on the way to building your strategy for successful cold call selling.

Lee Boyan

Contents

1

Playing Your Tune

An Insight from a Dairyman

In the opening scene of *Fiddler on the Roof,* Tevye the dairyman steps to the front of the stage to set the mood for the musical. He pauses for a moment, surveys the audience, hitches up his trousers, and speaks a few lines that every salesperson can relate to: "A fiddler on the roof? Sounds crazy, no? Every one of us is a fiddler on the roof, trying to scratch out a simple tune without breaking his neck."

Everyone who makes a living in sales is like Tevye's fiddler, perched precariously on the ridgepole, high above the comfortable and safe anonymity of the crowd, exposing his or her precious ego to the winds of indifference, preoccupation, skepticism, and sometimes outright rejection.

The Wallflower Syndrome

Can you remember your early high school dances as well as I? Especially the ones that took place about the time you were a sophomore and which caused so much anxiety? The girls would line up along one wall while the boys would stand along the other wall with their hands in their pockets, their Adam's apples bobbing nervously.

It mattered little that the band played well the catchy tunes of the time. Or that the bandleader joked with the boys and girls,

1

trying to get the boys to move out from the wall, to cross that forbidding no-man's land, to ask the girls to do what everyone there was eager to do. The only kids dancing were those already going steady, some girls dancing together, and a few fellows who had somehow learned that you often get from life what you ask for. But when the closing theme song faded away, most of the sophomores were still firmly anchored against the wall—girls on one side, boys on the other, frozen in place by a paralyzing fear that a fragile, young ego may get bruised by rejection.

They don't change much as years go by. There are thousands of salespeople glued behind their desks or behind the wheels of their cars, stuck in place by the awesome fear of asking a prospect to dance a few steps. Instead of playing a tune like the fiddler on the roof, they spend time and energy hanging on to the roof. Shakespeare expressed our fears of rejection very well: "Our doubts are traitors and make us lose the good we might achieve by fearing the attempt."

There it is, spelled out for us hundreds of years ago, by one of the world's most perceptive authors. We all protect our egos, frequently by avoiding the very opportunities that would make us feel great about our abilities and worth.

How Cold Is a Cold Call?

Most salespeople prefer to have business come easily, for example, as repeat orders from regular customers, response from advertising, or inquiries. Those certainly are ideal sources, but it requires less sales ability to get that kind of business than it does to make unsolicited approaches to strangers who are proper buying authority.

In the vernacular of the sales profession this is known as a cold call. That term itself can be part of the problem which makes this type of call seem difficult for too many salespeople. One dictionary lists these synonyms for the word *cold:* inhospitable, unsociable, unwelcome, forbidding, unfriendly, ungracious, uncordial, unapproachable. I can just see someone identifying with those definitions and adding, perhaps subconsciously, this one—unworthy of my time and risk to my sensitive ego.

A Roadblock to Be Removed

The problem is not just that most salespeople prefer business to come in the easy way. The commonplace yet subtle reality is—fear. Fear of possible rejection in that seeming inhospitable, unsociable, unwelcome, forbidding, unfriendly, etc., territory. Fear of appearing awkward and feeling embarrassed in an unpredictable personal encounter.

In my experience working with salespeople in the field, I've met countless who have all the tools to become outstanding. They have the intelligence, looks, pleasing personality, and product knowledge but they don't put those gifts to full use because of fear of the threat to their ego. They prefer to call on a familiar friendly customer who may not offer the sales potential of prospects more difficult to get in to see. They spend more time than necessary in the office setting up calls, shuffling through prospect cards, or in the car traveling from one call to another—and passing all kinds of good prospects along the way. It is easier to sit comfortably behind the wheel, listening to the stereo, watching the scenery go by, than it is to be face to face with a prospect and risk rejection. It is easier to justify some kind of work activity being done, even if it's not productive. As I've often heard, "Gee, I left the house at 7:00 A.M., didn't get back until 9:00 P.M." But most of the time was spent driving. The only people who get paid for driving automobiles are chauffeurs and cab drivers. They usually don't get paid very much. Of course, there is necessary distance to travel between calls and the urgency of a prospect ready to buy may determine the travel distance. But the issue here is to be honest with ourselves—are we avoiding a perceived risk of rejection, are we hanging on to the roof instead of playing our tune?

The Underlying Cause of Call Reluctance

The need to gain approval of others is buried deep in the human psyche. We are conditioned by this need from infancy. As helpless children we really needed acceptance from our parents. Later the need for acceptance became the need for approval—when we learned there was a reward (approval) when we behaved as our parents wanted us to behave and there was punishment (disapproval) when we didn't. Later still, we conformed to values and behavior of our peers. To not be approved by them was to suffer feelings of rejection that our tender, young ego could hardly bear. In school much of what we learned was motivated by seeking approval of the teachers and authority figures. On our first job it soon became clear to us that the way to get along, to keep the job, to get a raise in pay, to get promoted was to gain approval of our boss. The dating and mating game totally revolves around approval not only of our dates and mates but also of their friends, our relatives, and especially our future in-laws. This is not to speak disparagingly of parents, teachers, bosses, and in-laws. I've served my time as the approver in enough of those roles. That is just the way it is. It's part of the human condition in our society. It has been that way for a long time and probably isn't going to change in the foreseeable future.

But this urge for approval does affect our feelings and resulting performance on our job in the sales profession. It shows up especially when we have to risk taking the initiative to announce our presence and state our business to a prospect who is a stranger and who is preoccupied with other important matters. Rare indeed is the individual who takes that risk calmly, naturally, without proper conditioning or training to counteract the ingrained effect of a lifelong pursuit of approval. It is the purpose of this book to provide you with a course of action that will give you that kind of conditioning and training.

Rarely do sales training programs deal with the subject of fear. From my discussions with sales executives, I find that the reason it is avoided is that it is considered to be negative. I don't buy that. Positive thinking doesn't mean that you close your eyes to reality. Much has been said about how easy it is to sell, how quickly money can be made, "all you gotta do is act enthusiastic, etc., etc." All of which often doesn't connect with what is going on in the solar plexus of the salesperson standing before an indifferent, preoccupied, sometimes unfriendly prospect. I believe it is a positive approach to train salespeople how to accept the reality of fear and how to deal with it. The next chapter will show you how.

2

Triumph over Fear

Admitting Fear

The starting point for building skill in making uninvited initial contacts with prospective buyers is to recognize, admit, and then control the normal fear of disapproval and rejection. To deny it is to set in motion all sorts of immobilizing defense mechanisms.

Most salespeople experience fear. It's nothing to be ashamed of. So be honest. Bring fear out into the open. Then go to work to deal with it. There is no legitimate reason for anyone to deny the normal emotions all salespeople feel at one time or another. Admit you don't like to call on people who don't want to see you. And you don't relish talking about something you feel they don't want to talk about. That's natural. We all have an ebb and flow to our feelings and to our ambition.

What You Can Control

As you prepare to deal with the fear of rejection there are two important considerations to keep in mind. The first is: *What is actually going on in the world of that prospect?*

Your prospect may have recently learned of a serious complaint from a customer. Maybe a key employee just resigned. There could be a difficult personal problem or any one of endless possibilities to preoccupy his or her attention. Perhaps there was a recent experience with an inept or dishonest salesperson. It could be the

5

prospect is by nature suspicious or surly—or, just maybe, is a friendly person in need of your product and eager to see you!

The second consideration is: *How do you interpret and respond to what is going on?* Number one, the fact that the people you call on are preoccupied with immediate problems, or have difficult personalities, or must deal with whatever may be going on in their world, cannot be changed by you. Of course, a skillful sales approach can lessen any negative consequences. This book will tell you how.

Number two is different. That can be changed. You personally have the universal human ability to choose how you interpret and respond to any situation you face. And this includes how you interpret and respond to whatever may be going on in the world of your prospect.

Meaning from Horror

Dr. Viktor Frankl is a reknowned Austrian psychiatrist who spent three years in Nazi concentration camps during World War II, and wrote a book about his experiences entitled *Man's Search for Meaning*. The first part of the book described in vivid detail the ghastly horror of concentration camp existence. The second part explained an important discovery he made about human nature. Despite the incredible suffering he witnessed—the brutality, the lack of sleep, the overwork, the hunger, the ever-present specter of the gas chambers—he observed that everything can be taken away from human beings except what he called the last of the human freedoms. And that is freedom to choose one's attitude in any given situation.

He remembered how some few prisoners would walk through the barracks trying to comfort the others, trying to keep up their spirits, trying to ease if only a little bit the dreadful circumstances they found themselves in. He also noticed that the prisoners who behaved this way were in a very small minority. Most prisoners simply gave up. They bemoaned their difficult situation, and that only made them feel worse. Then he also noticed that the difference between these two kinds of behavior was the result of an inner decision that a person made and not a result of the camp influence alone. For they were all exposed to exactly the same exterior circumstances. He also noticed that the ones who took the positive outlook were the ones who survived. They survived incredible stress.

We don't live in circumstances anywhere near what they had to go through in concentration camps. Yet, how many times a day are we faced with situations where that choice, that inner decision, will determine our circumstances, our relationships with other people, and how we're going to feel.

A Failure Turned into Success

Anna Mae Randall sells an air freight service to customers in Fort Worth. Her customers regularly ship small but valuable cargo from Texas all over the world. One day early in the week she called on a new prospect and persuaded the traffic manager to use her company's service for shipping oil well drilling equipment spares frequently needed by drillers in Saudi Arabia, Mexico, the North Sea, and other distant locations. It showed promise of being an excellent account and Anna Mae felt so sure of it that she started phoning other prospects to set up a series of calls for the rest of the week. On Friday she didn't bother to go to her office but went straight to work making her calls. As a result, she didn't learn that the drilling company equipment manager had called to cancel his agreement.

Not knowing about the defunct order, Anna Mae continued working with high expectations. She had the assurance of a success-ful salesperson and got several more orders. When the day was over she drove home, still without checking in at the office. She later said:

> It was the best weekend in years. My husband and I went out on the town to celebrate. I called my boss, who congratulated me on my best week ever. It wasn't until Monday morning that he and I learned that the oil well equipment order had been canceled. I discovered that the success which turned me on for the rest of the week was a failure. By then it didn't matter because the others

were so much better. Funny, it was that first order I thought I had and really didn't, that made me get out and hustle to sell still more. Yet, I recall another time I'll have to admit, when a canceled order made me feel so bad, I went into a slump that lasted several weeks.

When Anna Mae told me that, I could only think how important our reactions are and how unimportant our individual failures are when we just do the work we should be doing. When her perceptions were that she was successful, she became successful. When she perceived failure, she made it happen.

How to Control Emotions

It is important to understand that we, like Anna Mae, choose our own response to what is happening to us. Choosing a response begins with an interpretation. That is, we use words to explain what we perceive to be going on. We do this verbalizing mentally as self-talk or as we explain it to others. Now we are at the heart of where critical choices are made. We *choose* the words in our interpretation. The words trigger our feelings and actions, which in turn determine what happens to us.

Psychologist Albert Ellis, who has written many books on psychology in language that a lay person can understand, expressed the concept this way: "One has enormous control over one's emotions if one chooses to work at controlling them and to practice saying the right kind of sentences to oneself." And Dr. Maxwell Maltz added this in his popular book *Psycho-Cybernetics:* "Ideas are changed, not by 'will,' but by other ideas."

Harnessing the Power to Change

We have the power to replace faulty ideas and wrong assumptions with more constructive ideas when we are aware of this power. Most intelligent people will agree with the axiom that positive thoughts bring positive results and negative thoughts bring negative results. That is, they agree with the concept when they are reading a book or sitting in a seminar on the subject, but that awareness quickly evaporates and often it is not there in the routine, workaday world.

It's like the monks who took a vow of silence in their cloistered monastery. This vow was relaxed once a year on Christmas morning when they were free to greet each other, to praise God aloud, or to share their feelings that had been suppressed all year. One Christmas morning as they were taking turns speaking, a young monk at the end of the table spoke. "The oatmeal is cold." No one responded since the brothers all had better use for their rare privilege.

Another year passed in total silence except for the necessary orders from the Brother Superior in making work and worship assignments. Again, on Christmas morning as the brothers were exchanging greetings, the little brother at the bottom of the table looked up in disgust, pushed his bowl away, and repeated, "The oatmeal is cold." Still no one answered him.

Yet one more year passed in near total silence and once more at the Christmas breakfast table, amid the brotherly greetings, came the now familiar wail. "The oatmeal is cold."

In the silence that followed, the Brother Superior rose with a look of intense disappointment on his face. He sadly shook his head and pointed to the door. "Brother Aloysius, you have done nothing but complain for three years so I'm sending you home. We are sick and tired of this griping, griping, griping!"

People who habitually choose negative statements in their inner dialog and in their communication with others seldom realize the damaging power negative choices have upon their lives.

In the Beginning Are the Words

Often in my consulting practice I hear people explain away poor performance with a logical excuse. They will say, "Our business is different." Then they'll describe problems unique to their business over which they have no control. Yet there are others in the same kind of business with the same set of problems who are doing great! No matter how logical, excuses never have anything to do with the solution to a problem. The solution to a problem must begin with constructive words in the mind and on the lips of the would-be problem solver.

What You Can Learn with Your Eyes Closed

There is another important way that ideas can be changed. For example, I will give you the word *beach*. Now put the book down for about 30 seconds and close your eyes.

What did you see in your mind's eye? White sand? A pounding surf? Sailboats in the distance? Sunbathers lying on beach blankets? Children making sand castles? Or whatever picture recalled from your own experience on a beach? Or did you picture the word B-E-A-C-H?

Most likely you pictured familiar scenes that the word *beach* evoked in your mind rather than the word. As important as words are in representing ideas, mental pictures are also important, sometimes more so. You can control the pictures that dwell in your mind as well as the words. For centuries philosophers have been telling us that we tend to act out the pictures we allow in our minds. Recently their philosophical musings have been proved in studies using scientific methods.

The Mental Dynamics of a Sales Call

Now let's see how the choice of words and pictures can affect the performance of a salesman making an unsolicited call on a stranger. Let's call him Harry.

Harry represents a printing firm that specializes in high-quality color reproduction for large-volume clients. Harry is about to make a call on a mail-order merchandiser who has been having catalogs and brochures printed by a competitor.

On the way to his destination, Harry is thinking, "Boy, I sure hate making these cold calls. Maybe I'd better stop for a cup of coffee and figure out how to handle this situation."

He recalled that a salesman who previously called on Mr. Bullman, the advertising manager of the mail-order house, said he was a hard-nosed character. Harry's stomach begins to churn! He envisions a gruff-looking individual impatiently meeting him in the reception lobby. He imagines the embarrassment he suffers as Mr. Bullman makes quick work of his rejection out loud in front of other waiting salespeople.

Harry wishes he were about to call on a friendly, familiar customer and begins to wonder if it might be better to do just that instead. But his manager has been after him to get some new accounts. In fact, a quarterly performance review is coming up soon and he will have to make an accounting of himself. That could be more painful than facing Mr. Bullman.

His stomach churns some more! Then he recalls reading somewhere that people always respond to us the way we expect them to respond to us. So expect a positive reception.

"Well," he muses, "that doesn't always work. Matter of fact, the last few cold calls did not turn out to be very positive greetings. There must be something wrong with me. I don't seem to be able to positive-ize my expectations."

Now Harry is back to square one with the churnings in the pit of his stomach. So he grits his teeth and goes out to make the call despite the fear of being hurt and humiliated. He's like the comic strip character, good ole Charlie Brown, who is up to bat in the bottom of the ninth with two outs and his team behind 60 to 0. But this is not the kind of emotional state for Harry to be in to perform at his best.

How could Harry have changed his interpretation of this scenario?

To begin with, Harry didn't know the kind of reception he was actually going to get from Mr. Bullman. It could be warm and friendly. It could be indifferent. It could be hostile. So his first mistake was to make an assumption that was extreme. In this case it was extreme—negative. That assumption was biased with someone else's opinion. Opinions are not usually a good source of objective reality.

Harry was right not to take the other extreme, that is, to expect a positive reception. But of course, he knows better. He's been burned with that one before.

Effective Prejudgment

It would make most sense for Harry to choose to expect a neutral reception—neither especially warm nor especially cool. The law of averages dictates that that is most likely the way it will actually be.

It comes with the territory. It is normal. It's all in a day's work if taken in stride. Of course, he would *prefer* the prospect to be agreeable. But if not it's no big deal.

We allow ourselves to become upset when people don't behave the way we want them to. To make matters more upsetting, according to a prevalent false notion in traditional sales lore, we should be able to manipulate them into behaving the way we want. When that doesn't happen we feel inadequate. Brooding over this negative self-judgment further inhibits our ability to perform. It can even immobilize us.

On any given call, chances that you would meet with a difficult prospect are very slight. Even if you did, whatever happened would not ruin your sales career.

It's a fact of life, especially in selling, that people often don't act the way we want them to act. How do we perceive this—as a threat or an opportunity? That is a choice we make. Do we make that choice consciously and deliberately? Or do we allow ourselves to be controlled by negative habit patterns?

An Old Pro Reveals the Secret of Security

I will never forget Ben Moore. Ben was the manager on my very first sales job selling cookware direct to the consumer. It's not the easiest product in the world to sell but it's good for learning how to sell. After a couple of weeks, I hadn't sold a thing. A lot of doors were slammed in my face. Dogs chased me down the street. I had blisters on my hands from carrying those big, heavy sample cases.

One day at lunch I ordered tea and toast. (I was about 20 pounds lighter then than I am today.)

"You're a pretty skinny guy to be on that kind of diet," the waitress remarked.

"I'm not on a diet. But I'll tell you what I am on. I'm on commission. That's what I'm on."

I went to Ben with my crying towel out. "Ben, I'm just not cut out for this commission selling. There's no security in it."

That struck a nerve. Ben came back to me with, "Security? What are you talking about? Security is how you can do this here job—

how you can sell this here cookware. Security is in yourself, boy. Ain't no other place. Security is how you can get in those doors being slammed at ya. Security is how ya gets people to sit down and listen to ya when they're too busy. You'll get yourself a whole bunch of security when you gets people interested in this cookware after they tells ya they're not interested. Now get out there on the street with those sample cases and don't come cryin' to me about where there ain't no security."

The Great Opportunity

And that is so true. Resistance is the reason for the existence of the sales profession. It's the reason you get paid. And the more skillful you are dealing with it, the more you will get paid.

To start out the day wishing you won't run into any resistance, to look for prospective buyers who always greet you with open arms, is not being realistic. It's true you will meet agreeable buyers once in a while. But if they become too commonplace, you might be out of a job. Your company could get all the distribution it wants without the expense of a sales force. So fortunately for the sales profession, buyers aren't always that easy. Sometimes they will not be especially eager to see you at the particular time you happen to call, even though they could eventually become very interested and could profit from your offering. Such prospects can provide your best opportunities.

A Sure-Fire Method for Dissolving Fear

Despite their best efforts to do so, some salespeople have difficulty in avoiding images of hostile prospects. If you are affected this way, then it is best to make the image absurdly extreme.

One of my clients has an experienced field sales manager who is quite good at getting trainees to do this. Once, when the company was opening up a new territory, Ed Posnan was hired for his first sales job. Jack Davis, the manager, worked with Ed for two weeks before sending him out on his own. For the first week the older man did most of the work. He led Ed into likely businesses, introduced both of them to potential customers, and demonstrated the company line of building supplies. Jack made a good number of presentations, sold several new accounts, and laid a good foundation for Ed's follow-up calls. The young man watched, took many notes, and asked questions.

At the start of the second week, Jack instructed Ed to make a call by himself. He pointed out a factory that made prefabricated houses.

"This is the Thompson Company. I want you to go in, introduce yourself to Mr. Thompson, and present our line to him."

Ed gulped hard, stared at the building, but made no move.

"Tell me, Ed. Where are you now?"

The younger man looked confused by the question.

"Why, in your car in Thompson's parking lot."

"And what is the very worst thing that could happen if you call on Mr. Thompson today?"

Ed thought about that for a moment.

"I suppose he could swear at me for interrupting his work. He could refuse to hear my presentation. He might even have plant security escort me to the front door. I don't think they would throw me out bodily. Too much danger of a lawsuit in that these days."

Jack nodded thoughtfully. "And then where would you be?"

Ed started to laugh and then turned to get his case from the back seat.

"Right back here, sitting in your car in Thompson's lot."

"See?"

Ed laughed aloud and lifted his case from the back seat. "I think I'll go see if Thompson's guards are all that tough."

The procedure that Jack used with Ed was a modification of the process taught by Dr. Viktor Frankl, whom I've mentioned earlier. The famed psychiatrist calls it *paradoxical intention*. It is based on the principle that the harder we try not to think about something, the more difficult it is to forget it.

In the Middle Ages, charlatans would sell lead bars to gullible peasants with the guarantee that they would change into gold overnight, providing the purchaser *did not* think about becoming wealthy. It was a perfect catch-22 proposition. No one could spend the night waiting for lead to become gold without gloating about the good fortune and anticipated wealth. In the morning when the lead had not changed, the charlatan would accuse the poor sucker of not following instructions. And the peasant would have to admit that he had, indeed, thought about becoming wealthy.

The harder we try not to think about fear, the more it comes unbidden to mind. On the other hand, it is possible to embrace the fear, turn it into a ridiculous affair, and allow the normal human appreciation of the absurd to turn it off completely.

When paradoxical intention is used in therapy, people are instructed to conjure up their worst fears rather than to avoid them. They are to embrace them, to magnify them greatly, and to make them so absurd that their minds rebel at the ridiculousness of the images being created. Paradoxical intention can be used as an inner conversation with one's self or in an actual conversation with someone else.

Ed Posnan might have said something like this:

> I am getting ready to face up to Old Man Thompson. I am terrified because he is the meanest human being in history. Beside him, Hitler, Genghis Khan, and Nero are all choirboys. He is so cruel that he hires guards with tommy guns to keep his employees from storming the office during coffee breaks.

> Along the back wall of his office, stuffed and mounted like hunting trophies, are the heads of former salespeople who called on him. Of the last 200 men and women who tried to sell him anything, only one got away to tell how mean Thompson really is. He is so bad that his secretary is the former karate champion of Japan. She can handle him but I can't be expected to.

> I'm really going to bomb out. When I get in there, I'm really going to make a fool of myself. I'll be standing there before him, looking at all those heads mounted along the wall behind his desk, and I'll turn to a quivering mass of protoplasm. My knees will shake and I'll stammer like a sophomore at my first dance. He'll snarl at me, the fire and smoke will come from his mouth, and I won't be able to say a word. I'll be stricken so mute that I'll never be able to speak again to another prospect, even if I somehow make it out of there before he cuts off my head.

Just try telling something like that to a friend with a straight face! The absurdity is so obvious that the human mind will immediately reject it. For if there is anything that our minds appreciate, it is the patently ridiculous. Harvard psychologist Gordon Allport wrote that any person who can devise a way to laugh at his problems is well on the way to solving them. Once ridiculed thoroughly, they lose the power to tie the mind in a helpless knot.

Norman Cousins was suffering unending agony from what was diagnosed as terminal cancer. He discovered, however, that he could end his pain at will by watching old Laurel and Hardy movies until he had a belly laugh. Each spasm of laughter would end his pain for half an hour or more.

The absurdity of a paradoxical intention statement, which would seem to make the problem worse, invariably has the opposite result. Hence the term paradoxical. It actually deflates a fear by opening it to ridicule and exposing it for the fraud the fear really is. The human mind cannot contain both the fear and the ridiculous image the paradoxical statement calls up to consciousness. After all, if you have faced the possibility of having your head handed to you on a platter, however jokingly, nothing a customer can actually do will be serious by comparison.

The ridicule of the paradoxical intention should be directed at the fear and not at yourself. If your anxieties are too strong to use the technique by yourself, have a trusted friend speak the absurdities for you.

Dr. Jard DeVille, author of *Nice Guys Finish First*, has had considerable experience using paradoxical intention as a mental health process. He says: "Don't let the apparent simplicity of the process keep you from using it, since it is one of the most powerful psychological techniques ever developed. I have seen many people rid themselves of a lifetime of phobias in a few minutes with it."

Keeping Reality in Focus

Even if you do not go to the extent of thinking up absurdities, consider the worst thing that could actually happen to you on a call. Whatever words or pictures you use to describe it, logic will not permit you to include someone slapping your face, or calling the police, or throwing you out bodily. The worst possible thing that could happen, as with Ed Posnan, is that you would be right back where you started. You didn't have any business from that prospect before going in. You don't have any coming out. Nothing lost but a few minutes time and maybe a little injured pride.

Ask yourself what your objective is. Is it to avoid failure, or is it to achieve something significant? Is it to protect your ego, or is it to sell your product? Is it to maintain status quo, or is it to gain valuable experience?

A baseball player often swings a leaded bat just before his turn at the plate. This makes the regular weight bat seem easier by contrast. Likewise, if you get practice on tougher prospects and learn to deal with them effectively, the average ones will be a piece of cake.

A Plus Value—Growth

As you gain more experience, your confidence will grow. It will become easier. You will eagerly look forward to more such experience. Selling becomes real fun.

Success in your sales career is measured not only in immediate sales but also in your growing skill. In being better able to deal with all kinds of situations. Rejection and injured pride are transient. They will pass. Personal growth is permanent. It can never be taken away from you.

This growth happens as the cumulative effect of experience, day after day, call after call. But sometimes it comes in a flash of insight from one experience in particular. That can be a real turning point in your career and that can be exciting. It happened to me.

How to Deal with a Tough Prospect

Years ago I sold radio advertising. Being the newest member of the station's sales staff, I was assigned a list of business firms to call on which had very little previous record of spending any advertising dollars in radio. One prospect was a crotchety old auto dealer, who seemed to like to enliven dull afternoons by shaking up salespeople who came to call.

One afternoon he gave me a particularly rough going over. I was thoroughly psyched out. The next thing I remember I was standing on the sidewalk in front of his dealership scratching my head.

"Hoo boy, there's got to be a better way to make a living," I thought, as I was ready to throw in the towel.

It so happened I had had lunch a few hours earlier with a friend who told me a story that I now believe I was fated to hear that day. I really think that's the way it works. You get the help you need when you need it when you are immersed in what you're supposed to be doing.

Who Has the Problem?

The story concerned two businessmen who were in competition with each other. It was tough competitive business, and they just hated each other's guts. Each had his office in the same tall building, and every morning they would get on the elevator at the same time.

One was tall with a full head of hair. The other was short and bald. Every morning the tall one would stand behind the short one on the elevator and spit on his bald head. Every morning the short one would take a facial tissue out of his pocket and wipe his head off without saying a word.

A third man would also get on that elevator every morning at the same time. He watched this daily drama with a good deal of curiosity. After a couple of weeks he couldn't restrain his curiosity anymore.

"Tell me something, why do you let that guy get away with such a gross insult?" he asked the short man after the tall one got off the elevator to his lower-floor office.

"Well, you know that's his problem, not mine," the bald one replied.

Stop and think about that for a minute. When people are rude to us, even sometimes when they are unfair to us, it's really their problem, not ours. When we give them a taste of their own medicine, we're stooping to their level. It's better to pity people like that.

So there I was in front of this car dealership ready to throw in the towel and the meaning of that story jarred loose my self-pity. "Of course," I thought, "that car dealer has a problem, not me. He's sick, not me."

I recalled the days when I was a kid. The bully was never the toughest kid on the block. The bully acted that way because he was scared inside. It's the way he learned to keep other kids at a safe distance. Sometimes we see that bully behavior in a grownup. Psychologists tell us that such a person is the one who most fears rejection. Deep down he is timid. He adopts such obnoxious behavior in order to protect himself from the possibility of being hurt.

Unmasking the Toughness

But he does buy goods and services. He must, in order to keep his business functioning. Somebody is selling him. Salespeople who sell him don't mirror his unpleasantness. Nor do they come with hat in hand. In his heart the bully knows he has a weakness. Never mind how firmly he may deny it. In order to mask it, he will make a special effort to show his contempt for weakness in others.

Those who sell him understand that beneath the mask of antagonism is another kind of person, one who can be sold. And they penetrate his hard shell with understanding, with patience, and with a firm belief in the value of what they sell.

You don't change them, but the relationship changes. I realized I couldn't change that crotchety car dealer, but I could change my perception of him. I did just that right there on the sidewalk by merely feeling sorry for him. Once a genuine feeling of pity sank in, my fear of him and others like him evaporated.

Psychologist Erich Fromm explains in his book *The Art of Loving* what happens during this kind of change of perception:

> I may know that a person is angry, but I may know him more deeply than that. Then I know that he is anxious and worried—that he feels lonely—that he feels guilty. Then I know that his anger is only the manifestation of something deeper. I see him as anxious and embarrassed. That is as the suffering person, rather than the angry one.

Now it didn't happen that I went back in and sold the car dealer a big contract. But there were others down through the years that were sold. Lacking this newly gained insight, I might have been tempted to shy away from them. I surely would have hated to subtract those commissions from my earnings, to say nothing of the self-esteem that would have been surrendered along the way.

It pays to cultivate customers like Mr. Obnoxious. Once you get through to him, you have a loyal customer. Your competition will be having a problem with Mr. Obnoxious.

Getting Rid of Irritation and Frustration

Robert Conklin, creator of the "Adventures in Attitudes" program and author of a recent best-seller on personal growth entitled *How to Get People to Do Things*, offered this insight in an earlier work, *The Dynamics of Successful Attitudes:* "We usually form opinions about how other people should act. Then we sit in constant judgment of them. Each time they do not conform to one of our molds, we pull the trigger of one of 5,000 irritations and frustrations."

This means that the irritations, the frustrations, and the fear are self-imposed. We choose to activate them within ourselves. We could choose, instead, not to activate them, by tempering our judgments and by changing our perception. Then we would be in a much stronger position, emotionally, to deal with the stress we are exposed to in the sales profession.

Preparing a Solid Foundation

Whenever the stresses build up after a series of disappointments, read this chapter again. Ponder how the ideas suggested in it would apply to individual calls that you made. Put yourself into the situations of the salespeople in the examples. The ability to use your power of choice is a skill. As with any skill, it will improve with practice. Practice the technique of changing your mental words and pictures as suggested in this chapter until it becomes second nature. This will prepare a solid foundation to your complete strategy for developing new business. You will build on this foundation in the following chapters.

3

What Do You Want to Happen?

It Begins with an End

"In a nutshell, I can tell you the difference between my top producers and the ones just getting by," a sales manager once told me. "My top producers are motivated by a desire for pleasing results. The mediocre ones are motivated by a desire for pleasing methods. And they will settle for whatever results their comfortable way of operating will bring."

The idea of setting objectives, of making clear-cut decisions on exactly what results you want, is not a new idea in personal motivation or in business, in selling in particular. You can hardly pick up a book on the subject of selling without a chapter on goal setting, or attend a sales seminar where it isn't an important part of the agenda. If you've been in the sales profession for any length of time, chances are you've been required to put in writing some kind of forecast of what you expect to accomplish.

This chapter is not intended to be a primer on the subject of goal setting. Rather, its purpose is to point out the importance of making clear-cut definitions of and commitments to exactly what we want to accomplish in getting new business.

People Resist Change

It is reasonable to assume you are reading this book in order to bring about a change that results in new business. To keep doing what you have been doing in the past will only bring the same kind of results as in the past. In order to bring about a change in results, you must do things differently. This is not easy. Often those who want the benefits change will resist doing what is necessary to make it happen.

I used to play the accordian years ago, back in the days when accordians were popular. In fact, I made a living at it for a while, but it doesn't get played much anymore. Occasionally, when we are entertaining friends, someone will insist I bring it out and play a few tunes.

"You must get a lot of enjoyment out of playing an instrument like that," somebody will usually remark.

"Matter of fact, I don't," is my standard reply. "I can't play it the way I used to. I know what the music is supposed to sound like. But I just can't make the fingers do it anymore."

"Lee, you're crazy not to play that accordian more often," a friend once said. "I'd give anything to play a musical instrument like that. You know, I've always wanted to play the guitar. I love to sing. So then I could sing and play the guitar, and that'd be great."

"Are you serious about that?" I asked.

"Of course I am."

"Well, consider it done." I gave him a sheet of paper and a pencil and said, "Now write this down: 'I will buy a guitar next week.' "

He wrote that down. "Now write this down: 'I will take lessons on this guitar starting next week.' "

He wrote that down. "Now this: 'I will practice playing that guitar 30 minutes a day starting next week.' "

After staring at his written words silently for several minutes, he crumpled up the sheet and threw it in the wastebasket.

Yes, there is a price to pay for bringing about change in one's life. Sometimes people are unwilling to pay it even though there can be a far greater price to pay for not changing. The choice must be made.

The process of setting goals accomplishes a sifting through the choices. Most people never learn that process. They may hear or read about it, but they fail to assimilate the meaning of it in their own lives.

Endlessness

"A big mental health problem today is boredom," said one psychiatrist. "It's not the routine, which most people blame, that causes the boredom. It's the endlessness of what they are doing. They just never seem to arrive at any particular destination. They never seem to get anywhere simply because they don't know where they want to go." They are like Alice in Wonderland.

> "Would you tell me, please, which way I ought to go from here?"
> "That depends a good deal on where you want to get to," said the Cat.
> "I don't much care where—" said Alice.
> "Then it doesn't matter which way you go," said the Cat.

Ridiculous, isn't it? And most people in the audience laugh at Alice when I tell that story in my seminars. It is ridiculous when you are talking about Alice in Wonderland. But it is tragic when you are talking about real people—and their lives.

Going Through the Motions

People in an organization that is being managed by some sort of formalized goal-setting program resist the goal-setting discipline also. As a consultant, occasionally I'm called in to be a trouble shooter on a management by objectives program that isn't working too well. The first thing I look for is participants just going through the motions, that is, filling out forms because their boss expects it of them.

Just before the quarterly performance review, there is a scramble to find the forms, which had not been looked at since they were filled out. Then creative energy is spent thinking up excuses why the job wasn't done. There is no commitment to the completion of those objectives.

Believe in the Concept of Setting Goals

In cases where the organizational goal-setting programs are working to good effect, I find that commitment flourishing—not only a commitment to the stated objectives, but also a commitment to the concept of goal setting as a way of life. The participants believe in it. They apply the goal-setting procedures in their personal and family lives as well as on the job.

It is even more important for salespeople to apply this principle. They must be self-starters, self-motivated. They don't punch a time clock or have constant supervision. The principle of goal setting has special meaning in making new contacts if there is any resistance to change or fear of rejection. It is human nature to do what is pleasant and avoid doing what is not. Goals will keep you on course—keep you doing what is necessary for successful achievement regardless of whether or not you like the necessary activities. Goals will keep you from going off in directions you had not intended to go and wasting valuable time.

Another important reason why goals are essential to cold call selling is that this phase of selling requires a good deal of creativity. Things must be made to happen from scratch!

The human brain is a super scanning device. When goals are clear, antennas go out. You will see and hear things that otherwise would be missed. The things you see and hear will have a different meaning as they apply to what you want to happen, and you will be able to make use of them.

The brain is also a super computer. Setting goals is the way it is programmed. Goals are the input. Creative ideas and solutions to problems are the output.

The wisdom underlying that concept is not particularly new. It was understood by King Hammurabi in ancient Babylon around 1750 B.C. At that time there was a problem with stone buildings collapsing and occupants getting killed. King Hammurabi put out an edict that declared, "If a building collapses and any occupant is killed, the builder will be put to death!" It is easy to imagine how creative the Babylonian builders became, figuring out how those buildings were to be built, once they knew exactly what they had to achieve.

Three Elements Necessary for Change

Observations from my training and consulting practice of thousands of salespeople and managers on the job have convinced me that change just does not take place without all three of these elements:

1. A clear definition of exactly what is to change.
2. A firm commitment to make it happen.
3. An action plan to carry it out.

The Definition

Here are vital points for defining a goal.

1. *Put it in writing*. We often think of writing as a means of communicating with other people. But what we write can be more enlightening to ourselves than to others. We can hold endless numbers of words in thought. Writing them down is a process of editing thoughts into their essential meaning. This avoids conflicting aims. If you choose to go north, you give up all possibility of going south for the time being. Sometimes this is not clear until it is written. Writing also keeps us honest. We are less likely to kid ourselves in writing. Like my friend who thought he wanted to play the guitar. When he wrote it down the truth came out. He was not willing to pay the price to learn.

2. *Quantify it*. Avoid vague statements such as, "My goal is to get some new business." You could get one new account that ordered a token amount of your product over a year's period of time and that goal, as stated, would have been achieved.

To make your goal statements positive affirmations, put them in the *past* tense, and quantify them: "To have sold 20 new accounts with total volume of $200,000." A quantified statement has numbers in it. Without numbers there is no way to recognize when the goal is achieved. The numbers also serve as measurements to check your progress. You can identify where you may need help or extra effort. The numbers also serve as a motivating force reminding you specifically of what it is you want to accomplish. The real world is brutally specific. Vague, wandering generalities just don't make contact with the real world.

3. *Date it*. Include in your goal statement the date you expect to achieve your goal. People resist doing this. It can be disturbing, even frightening—because it imposes a deadline responsibility for making it happen. Undated goals are meaningless. Not setting a time limit indicates a lack of decisiveness about reaching the goal. It is always off in some misty future. You are like the donkey with a carrot on the stick. It's always out there in front of you, but you never get to it.

A complete, written goal statement that is quantified and dated would read: "To have sold 20 new accounts with total volume of $200,000 by December 31." A written definition that is quantified and dated is a precondition for the next step.

The Commitment

Recently one of my clients had me fly to a sales meeting site in one of the company aircraft. To my surprise it was a single-engine plane.

"Isn't this unusual?" I asked the pilot. "I've flown in a lot of corporate aircraft and this is the first single-engine job I can recall." He replied:

> Well, most people feel safer in a twin-engine plane. They figure if one engine quits, you have another one to keep you up. But consider this. It takes a lot more pilot skill to keep a single-engine aircraft flying. It's terribly unbalanced. It's especially tough in bad weather. Worse, if you have to make a forced landing in bad weather.
>
> But pilot skill is only part of it. The real reason you may want to consider a single-engine airplane safer is this. If that engine quits, the pilot is totally committed to land that bird. There is no other option. Total attention, skill, and effort are concentrated on bringing it down as gently as possible. No distractions.
>
> A twin-engine pilot, no matter how skilled, isn't applying all of that skill to the one critically important task. A twin-engine pilot's mind is going back and forth struggling with a dilemma: Should I keep it up? Should I bring it down?

It occurred to me that people go through life like that. They never make a clear-cut decision—a commitment, so they can concentrate all of their energy, attention, and skill to it.

Commitment casts aside the self-imposed barriers encountered in making new contacts, such as procrastination and fear of rejection. It activates the inner creative mechanism which penetrates and resolves prospect resistance. It thus drives a person to a level of attainment beyond that which could ordinarily be expected from previously demonstrated ability.

A written definition that is quantified and dated is a precondition for commitment. One doesn't become committed to vague ideas. First, make a decision of exactly what it is you want to happen. Then make a second decision expressed here as inner dialog.

Say to yourself with meaning and conviction, "Yes, this is what I am going to do." That is the essence of commitment.

The Action Plans

Although goals are the source of motivating power, their realization does not happen automatically. They must be followed up with an action plan. Action plans translate goals into a step-by-step blueprint telling how the goals will be reached.

Salespeople are not inclined to be avid planners. For one thing, they are likely to be extroverts, and extroverts don't like routine. Planning is routine. Then too, plans have a way of being aborted. You make plans for a day when one of your biggest customers calls with a problem. You drop the carefully made plans to put out a brush fire. Other emergencies happen frequently. But all the reasons you hear from salespeople why they can't plan are actually reasons why they should plan.

Planning is often referred to as *time management*. I've never particularly liked the term time management because we really can't manage time. The clock ticks on relentlessly and nothing that we can do will change its precise, measured progression. We can manage only ourselves. I believe the reason that so many of us are lacking in self-management skills is that we never got into the habit of practicing such skills early. Most of us began our working careers in a job at which we were paid by the hour. And to reinforce the abandonment of our self-management, we punched a time clock.

The time clock then became a very important center of attention. It managed us. It determined the design of our day. It determined the size of our paycheck. Punch in, punch out—the number of hours on the time card times the hourly rate was it. For the most part, the power to decide what we would get done while we were there was given to someone else. Our only responsibility was to be there. Punch in, punch out. We got paid, regardless. We developed a mental habit of thinking about our job as a block of time to be filled with activities. These activities would then satisfy the time clock requirements, which justified our paycheck and our value to the organization that paid us. We tended to focus on activities rather than results.

In the sales profession, responsibility for results shifts to the salesperson. This includes responsibility for planning how the results will be made to happen.

The Key Fundamental—Priorities

There are many excellent books, courses, and programs on planning, or time management. Although each may suggest different methods, they all have a common, key element. That has to do with some method of identifying and setting *priorities*.

People usually have more things they would like to do or feel they ought to do than they have time to do. So they must choose. To set priorities is to make choices. Suppose you live in Chicago and choose to go to New York, you give up all possibility of going to Los Angeles at the same time. That is obvious. It is also a hypothetical situation. But without planning, we often place ourselves in similar incongruous situations in real life.

How to Determine Priorities—Force Field Analysis

A logical method for determining priorities is known as force field analysis. First, write out your goal statement at the top of a sheet of paper. Draw a line down the center. On the lefthand side directly under the goal statement write the words *Helping Forces*. On the righthand side similarly write the words *Hindering Forces*. Now on the lefthand side write everything you can think of that is helping you to achieve the goal. For example, it could be strong personal characteristics you have, advantages your product has over competitors', people you have to work with, sales aids your company provides. Do some creative brainstorming, and write down anything you can think of. Work for a quantity of items tangible or intangible that could help you reach your goal. If you need more than one sheet—fine. Keep writing as long as the ideas flow.

Now on the righthand side write down all the things you can think of that prevent you from achieving the goal. The completed form would look something like Figure 1. Write them down as they occur to you. At this stage there is no need to list them in order of importance. Explore your feelings, especially those that would go under hindering forces. Be honest about this. To deny emotional reasons that hinder you from achieving something does not stop their hidden, damaging effect. Just to admit them in writing so you can face them squarely will help to neutralize them.

Figure 1. Force field analysis.

Goal: To have sold 20 new accounts with total volume of $200,000.00 by December 31.

Helping Forces	*Hindering Forces*
1. Strong desire to achieve this goal.	1. Feel uncomfortable making new calls.
2. Territory with good potential.	2. Competitors are deeply entrenched.
3. Products with the following competitive advantages: a. b. c. d.	3. Our prices generally higher than competition's.
	4. Have been unable to reach key buying authority in high-potential accounts.
4. Benefits to the customer: a. b. c. d.	5. Servicing present customers is time-consuming, doesn't allow much time for new prospect calls.
5. Visual sales aids.	
6. Good advertising support.	
7. Supportive sales manager.	
8. Curiosity: I'm the new kid on the block!	

After completing your list of helping forces and hindering forces, write your goal statement at the top of another sheet of paper. Draw a line down the center. On the lefthand side write, "What I can do to maximize the helping forces." On the righthand side write, "What I can do to minimize the hindering forces."

Once again do some creative brainstorming and fill in each appropriate column with as many things as you can think of that would enable you to increase the positive effect of the helping forces and decrease the negative effect of the hindering forces.

You can do this exercise alone or with the help of your sales manager or another salesperson. It makes an excellent project for a sales meeting. Apply the rules of creative brainstorming. Aim for the largest quantity of ideas. As they flow, just write them down without making any judgments as to whether or not they are practical. Even silly ones should be encouraged. They can trigger your imagination for more useful possibilities. Use as many sheets for this as necessary.

Keep writing until you are reasonably sure your creative capacity is exhausted, then you can switch from the unrestricted, creative frame of mind to a judgmental one. Go back over your lists and refine them. Cross out the suggestions that are unusable. Narrow the lists down to essential items and arrange items in some order of importance. This can be done by assigning numbers to them or by arranging them in clusters, labeling each cluster A, B, or C according to their relative importance. Your Force Field Analysis is now complete. From this analysis you move on to the next step: developing a master action plan.

The Master Action Plan

The master plan is a list of subgoals, in order of priority, of all the things that need to get done in order to achieve the main goal. Figure 2 is an example of such a plan. Notice that once again the goal statement is written out at the top. The reason for that is to keep clearly in mind the original goal. Only eight items are shown in Figure 2 to show the form the master plan would take. It's likely you would have more items based on the final draft of your Force Field Analysis. The number in front of each item indicates relative priority.

Figure 2. Master action plan.

Goal: To have sold 20 new accounts with total volume of $200,000.00 by December 31.

1. Sell one new account each week, with average sale $10,000.00 projected for balance of the year.
2. Make 5 presentations to new prospects each week.
3. Add 10 new prospects to list each week.
4. List all accounts and prospective accounts in order of priority (to be completed by 8/10).
5. Set up itinerary geographically and proportion to account priority (to be completed by 8/15).
6. Write out telephone opening script (to be completed by 8/16).
7. Compose precall letter (to be completed by 8/17).
8. Send 10 precall letters each week (beginning 8/19).

The master plan provides a basis for your daily action plan. This is a list, again in order of priority, of the things you expect to get done that day. Notice the term "to get done" instead of "to do." Many people make up "to do" lists every day. "To do" lists are certainly better than no plan at all. But, the "to do's" tend to be activities, not end results. For example, making a call is an activity. Making a sale is an end result. Express your list in terms of end results rather than activities. In other words, a "to get done" list instead of a "to do" list. Like the builders of ancient Babylon, you will discover how creative you will be in figuring out what you need to do in order to accomplish what you want to get done. Get into the mental habit of thinking in terms of end results rather than being satisfied with filling your day with busy work.

There will be days when you will only finish one or two items on your lists. That's OK. If you start from the top of the lists, take heart from the fact that you are working on the highest priorities. The others will just have to wait. You may not get everything done you would like to by this method, but it wouldn't be possible to get them done at all any other way. If you don't have a method of consciously and deliberately committing your time to what you choose to be your highest priorities, it is most likely you will subconsciously gravitate to doing what is more pleasing, less risky, less difficult but also less important, less productive, less rewarding.

If all of this sounds like extra work, I would ask, compared with what? At first glance it may seem to be extra work compared with no planning at all. But good planning does not increase the workload. Instead, it helps you to work more effectively and productively with less physical effort. It's like the man chopping wood with a dull axe!

"Why don't you sharpen your axe?" a friend asked.

"I can't take the time to stop. It's taking me long enough to do this job as it is."

Ridiculous! Of course. But no more ridiculous than to launch into a day of selling without a clearly thought out plan of action. Do your planning during off hours—evenings or early in the morning before your selling day begins.

Some people fail in selling because of lack of product or technical knowledge. But many more people fail because they don't put the knowledge they have to profitable use. This is not to say that product knowledge isn't important. It is. It's like a hunting license. It gives you the right to your prospect's time and attention. But as a hunting license doesn't make you an expert marksman, product knowledge doesn't give you everything you need to effectively sell the product.

So often, among the top sales leaders on my clients' sales teams, I find persons with less than average formal education. They succeed because they know what they want to achieve, are committed to reaching their goal, have a game plan, and spend their time on their high priorities.

4

Where to Find Prospects

Beyond Enthusiasm

Some years ago I was engaged in hiring and training people to sell a sales training service to business firms. We would hire only one person in a given territory. That person was selected carefully on the basis of a proven set of criteria. When more than one candidate met these criteria, some of my personal bias would color the final decision. I leaned toward someone who showed a lot of enthusiasm for the program we were selling and who would seem to enjoy selling it. Usually those characteristics added a plus factor that would help a newcomer off to a successful start.

Jim Tucker (not his real name) checked out as an ideal candidate. He was a likable, intelligent young man who was quick to grasp the merit of our program. "This business is made to order for me. It's just what I've been looking for. I can't wait to get going on my own."

These and similar remarks I kept hearing during the first two days of my initial field training with him. It was a straight commission sales job with no salary or draw provided, so these remarks were nice for me to hear. Often a trainee's attitude would have a touch of "OK, show me it can be done." But Jim showed more eagerness and enthusiasm than most other trainees I had worked with.

The first two days were spent following up leads provided by Art

Anderson, who had the territory previously and recently retired. Wednesday noon after a quick lunch I took Jim to the public library to show him how to use various directories to identify prospects. Wednesday evening we went back to the library for a couple of hours digging up more prospects.

I impressed upon Jim the importance of using the hours between 8:00 A.M. and noon and between 1:00 P.M. and 5:00 P.M. to be in contact with prospects.

"These are the golden selling hours." I told him. "The hours when prospects are available are the only hours that pay off in commissions. Paperwork, library work, and planning are most profitably done at other times."

Jim was more quiet than usual as we drove from the library back to my hotel that evening. I guessed he was digesting all my sage advice.

The next morning when I awoke, the message light on my phone was blinking.

"Good morning, Mr. Boyan. There is an envelope in your box," was the cheery greeting from the hotel desk clerk. Here is what it said:

> Dear Lee:
>
> I will be unable to continue as a representative for your firm. I was called out of town for an important personal matter. I am sorry this happened. Thank you for your patience and your help.
>
> Sincerely,
> Jim Tucker

Several weeks passed before I was able to reach Jim by phone. It took a little probing before Jim finally admitted that he just couldn't see himself spending all that time digging through directories.

"I sincerely believe that you have the best program of its kind and one that is much needed by many companies. I wish I had used such a program when I first started my selling career. Your method of presenting it is just super, something I'd enjoy doing. But, Lee, the detail involved in looking up prospects kinda got to me," was Jim's wistful parting shot.

Jim's case may be somewhat extreme. Reason would suggest

that if he were as enthusiastic about the program and its presentation as he claimed to be, a certain amount of detail work would be endured in good spirits. But often people don't behave reasonably. There is a little bit of Jim in many salespeople when it comes to the nonselling detail work involved.

The first step in making a sale is finding someone to sell. At first glance this may seem obvious, but the best way to do it may not be readily apparent. In some selling situations, the prospects are easily identified. For example, a manufacturer of certain mechanical or electronic components would have a limited number of original equipment manufacturers who would have use for such components. The OEM prospects most likely would be well known in their trade. Companies that sell through a dealer or distributor organization may only occasionally need to replace or add customers. Dealers handling their products are easily spotted in the Yellow Pages of the phone book.

Become Prospect-Minded

For most salespeople, however, prospecting is a never-ending search in less conspicuous places. Gary Flaherty sells sales incentive and premium merchandising programs to business firms. He enjoys a very high income and is one of the tops in his field. When I asked him what single factor he felt contributed the most to his success, Gary explained:

> I'm not smarter than anybody, in fact I have only one year of college and didn't do too well there at that. And I'm not what you'd call a hard worker, but when I work, I want to spend that working time with the best prospects I can find. Now in order to do this I spend more time thinking about prospecting than any other phase of my job. The more I think about prospects the more good ones seem to turn up for me.

Here is a valuable lesson from a successful pro. Like Gary, become prospect-minded. Realize the importance of prospecting. Include in your action plans some time to develop and maintain a workable prospect file.

Suspects or Prospects

Prospecting is often thought of as the actual contact of potential customers, but before that can happen the potential customers must be identified. The act of simply accumulating names sometimes is referred to as suspecting. True prospecting involves gathering specific information that gives some indication of the likelihood that an individual or organization would be a buyer of your product or service. If you sell to business firms, the size of a company in terms of its annual sales or number of employees could tell you whether or not it is worth your time to make a call, because that information would tell you something about sales volume potential for your products there. Credit rating speaks for itself. Names of key individuals along with their titles give clues to where the buying authority may be. Other information will suggest which of your products or services can best satisfy their needs and how to approach them. A prospect, then, may be defined as someone who needs what you sell, can afford it, and has authority to buy.

If you sell direct to individuals or to families, you may have to devote more time to prospecting. In this case just getting names of suspects is easy. Any telephone book can give you all the names you want. But getting prospects with some degree of qualification is quite another task. Here your best source of prospects is from referrals from satisfied customers.

How to Get Referrals

The key word here is *satisfied*. The more satisfied your customers are, the higher the quality of leads you will get from them. Opportunities for giving customers satisfaction are great in direct selling because typically customers are not accustomed to having their satisfaction assured.

Think back over major purchases you have made of personal or household items such as automobiles, furniture, appliances, insurance, remodeling work, etc. Do you recall any time the salesperson came back after the sale was made to see if everything was satisfactory? Not too often, I'll bet. How do you feel about that?

On the other hand, how would you feel toward a salesperson

who did come back to see how well you were getting along with the investment you made? Suppose the salesperson gave you some ideas on how to make the greatest use of the product or how to take good care of it or otherwise showed genuine concern for your maximum satisfaction. Wouldn't you be more inclined to help that salesperson find other people who would be given similar care and concern for their satisfaction?

Yes, making after-the-sale follow-up and service calls is time wisely invested. Most salespeople in the direct, specialty field don't do it because of a mistaken notion that it is unproductive to do so. After all, the customer has already bought, and for a nonrepeat product, it is unlikely that customer will buy again for a while. And if the customer really isn't satisfied, all too many salespeople would rather avoid that confrontation. Yet, they should be the first to know if there is any kind of problem so it can be taken care of. Otherwise, the whole neighborhood and other acquaintances of the customer are likely to hear about it and be forever lost as prospects for the salesperson.

Referrals are also an excellent source of prospects for selling to business firms, institutions, and government units. Service calls are equally important in these markets. The nature of products and services sold to this sector usually require more follow-up calls, especially when repeat sales are a possibility. But for the very reason that follow-up calls happen here more often, salespeople frequently overlook the opportunity to ask for referred leads.

Persons of buying authority in the business and professional world maintain close contact with others of similar interest through trade and professional associations, service clubs, and other affinity groups. Be aware of these networks and of the opportunities they provide to add high-quality prospects to your file.

Please take special note of the words *high-quality*. You don't want just names, you want names of the best prospects that customer can give. So before you ask for referrals it is important to get your customer into a frame of mind that is conducive to giving you the best possible names. First make sure your customer is completely satisfied. Ask a few questions regarding how the product is being used, or about comments of other people involved with it. Of course, you are open to hearing a complaint or a problem, because if there is any dissatisfaction, what chance would you have of getting a good referral? On the other hand, here you are ready, willing, and eager to help your customer solve the problem.

Most likely there is no problem and you have a customer that is satisfied. Expand that satisfaction. Offer suggestions for even greater satisfaction. Ask questions about what it is that customer likes most about the product, the service, or dealing with you and your company. Try to get the customer's own words about a specific benefit. Often in the enthusiastic recounting of benefits the customer will volunteer names of others who should be enjoying the same benefits. But if not, now is the time to suggest there may be acquaintances of your customer who are missing out on those benefits. Or tell a story of another customer of yours who was struggling without the benefits until you came along and showed a better way. Make it clear that you are dedicated to helping people solve problems like that and there are, no doubt, a lot of them out there who could use your help.

Ordinarily, when a salesperson asks for referrals it sounds something like this: "Now that you are my customer, would you help me sell more of my product? I would appreciate the names of acquaintances of yours who would be prospects for me."

But you're going to be different. Your first order of business is helping others instead of yourself. Your emphasis and concern is not on selling products but on solving problems, on making life and business better for the friends of your customer. You are going to give those people the same kind of care and concern you have just demonstrated on that follow-up call. Now the customer is in the proper frame of mind to give serious thought to who would be the very best prospects for you and is more eager to make extra effort to help you contact these high-quality prospects.

Know Who You Are Looking For

It is important to develop a profile of who is your best prospect. Make a list of the best customers presently buying your product. Study this list. Look for the characteristics they have in common. When asking for referrals mention these characteristics to help the referrer think of names of people that match your profile. Be aware of those characteristics in all of your prospecting efforts. Some of the highest-paid salespeople such as Gary Flaherty are simply good qualifiers. They want to spend their selling time where it pays off most.

Referrals are an ideal source of prospects but by no means the only source. The highest expression of skill in selling is demonstrated in the ability to make effective contact with unknown prospects or with whatever knowledge is available through published reference data. If you depend entirely on referrals, you probably are not making the most profitable use of the best hours in the day for selling because there will be times you'll find yourself in certain locales with time to spare but no one to call on. An adequate supply of fresh prospects in your files will help you turn otherwise wasted time into profit. Here are some good places to find them.

Sources of Prospects

Dun's Marketing Services
Three Century Drive
Parsippany, NJ 07054

Million Dollar Directory, Volumes I, II, and III

Provides detailed information on 120,000 of the largest business firms in the United States, including headquarters locations, names of key executives, number of employees, and sales volume. Listings are shown alphabetically, geographically, and by product Standard Industrial Classification, known as SIC code number.

Billion Dollar Directory

Complements the *Million Dollar Directory* by identifying U.S. ultimate parent companies having large corporate families. Shows corporate family linkage and ownership of subsidiaries and divisions. In-depth corporate family listings appear alphabetically, geographically, and by SIC code number. These are supplemented by an extensive cross-reference index of divisions, subsidiaries, and ultimate parent companies.

Dun's Business Identification Service

Information on over 4,800,000 U.S. business establishments listed on microfiche cards. Each listing includes name of company, address, and headquarters or branch designation.

Dun's Marketing Services also publishes a metalworking industry directory, international directories, and other market profile analyses.

Contacts Influential
516 S.E. Norrison
Portland, OR 97214

Contacts Influential publishes directories of business firms in major metropolitan markets. The information provided includes size of firm; local, branch, or head office; length of time in business; SIC code numbers; and key people. The directories are updated monthly with new businesses, changes of ownership, moves, rumored moves, and personnel changes. All of the information is computerized so special selections can be made for specific types of accounts. For example, suppose you are in the insurance business and want to contact the small-group market—firms that have between 6 and 50 employees. Additionally, you don't want branch offices because you can't get approval from a branch and you don't want your competitors to know what you are doing so you want to delete other insurance companies. Contacts Influential can provide you with mailing labels for your mailing, 3 × 5 cards for follow-up, and printout for a control factor of just the firms you want.

Cole Publications
901 West Bond Street
Lincoln, NE 68521

Cole Publications' *City Cross-Reference Directory* provides detailed information in several categories.

1. Street Address Directory shows names of telephone subscribers listed by street address.
2. Numerical Telephone Directory shows name of each telephone subscriber according to the telephone number and whether business or residence.

3. Office Building Directory shows names, titles, and occupations of tenants in each office building.
4. City and Suburban Newcomer list shows new listings and new arrivals.
5. Family Income Level and Buying Power Guide shows average wealth and ratings on each street.
6. Census Tract Marketing Section shows census tract maps of the entire area including street guide, counts, and wealth rating for each tract.
7. Zip Code Marketing Section shows zip codes for the entire area including street guides and counts for each zip code.
8. Demographic Section enables you to select trade areas by median age, median number of persons per household, percentage of owner-occupied households, percentage of families with children under 12, median years of school completed, and a housing unit analysis.

Thomas Publishing Company
1 Penn Plaza
New York, NY 10119

Thomas Register of American Manufacturers

Eight volumes list companies alphabetically according to the products or services they manufacture. Two volumes list companies alphabetically by name along with address, zip code, phone number, branch office, capital rating, key executives, plus a brand name index. Six volumes are catalogs of companies.

Standard & Poor's Corporation
25 Broadway
New York, NY 10004

Three directories listing 37,000 corporations: 340,000 officers, directors, and other principals including an annual obituary listing; and separate listing of new individual and company additions.

R. L. Polk and Company
431 Howard Street
Detroit, MI 48231

Polk's City Directories

In addition to all large cities, Polk's series includes cities somewhat smaller than those included in the directories mentioned above. The directories identify occupations of some individuals and key executives of companies in the alphabetical section. A street address section lists principal occupants of each building, apartment, and office suite.

National Register Publishing Company
5201 Old Orchard Road
Skokie, IL 60077

Standard Classified and Geographical Directories

Both directories list 17,000 companies allotting annual appropriations for national or regional advertising campaigns, approximate annual sales, approximate number of employees, type of products sold, and key executives. The classified directory arranges companies in 51 product categories. The geographical directory arranges them by state and city. A trade name list identifies companies when only the trade name is known.

Directory of Corporate Affiliations

Shows the corporate structure of major U.S. companies, their divisions, subsidiaries, and affiliates, both domestic and foreign.

Prospector Research Services, Inc.
751 Main Street
Waltham, MA 02154

Sales Prospector

A newsletter giving information on new companies and company expansions and relocations.

Superintendent of Documents
U.S. Government Printing Office
Washington, D.C. 20402

U.S. Government Purchasing and Sales Directory

Lists the needs of the various government offices divided into military and nonmilitary spending.

John Wiley & Sons, Inc.
605 Third Avenue
New York, NY 10158

Directory of Federal Purchasing Offices

A listing of 130,000 government purchasers. Sections include agencies classified in groups by types of goods/services most frequently purchased, organization charts for all federal agencies, geographical listings identifying local purchasing offices, and a glossary of abbreviations and acronyms.

Directory Service Company
P.O. Box 9200
Boulder, CO 80301

For finding prospects in rural areas. Directory Service Company publishes county residence directories for 900 counties in the United States. A map of each township is included showing who lives where.

Standard Rate and Data Service
5201 Old Orchard Road
Skokie, IL 60077

Two volumes of over 500 pages with over 50,000 consumer and business mailing lists used in direct mail advertising will give you the source of lists of almost any classification of prospect you can imagine. SRDS also publishes directories of radio stations, TV stations, newspapers, business publications, and consumer publications.

Other Sources of Prospect Information

Yellow Pages of phone books are always handy. Most states publish directories of manufacturers and other business firms.

Chambers of commerce usually have rosters of local businesses. Some large-city industrial directories classify business firms by zip code, which helps you confine prospecting to a limited geographical area and so reduce wasted travel time. Local, regional, and national business magazines as well as the business section of local newspapers are excellent sources of information regarding personnel changes, new businesses, relocations, and expansions. Corporate annual reports are readily available giving depth information on key target prospects. Many industries, institutions, and organizations have nationwide directories. Trade and professional associations publish rosters of their memberships. Some trade magazines publish annual directory issues. Some sell their subscriber mailing lists.

If a source of information for your market has not been mentioned yet or you want to explore more possibilities, try this one:

Gale Research Company
Book Tower
Detroit, MI 48226

Directory of Directories

A reference guide of over 5,100 entries listing business and industrial directories, professional and scientific rosters, and all kinds of lists and guides. It lists 2,100 specific subject headings with cross references. Detailed information about each directory should enable you to make a decision about the probable usefulness or application of each publication.

Librarians are Willing Helpers

Many of the resources listed here are available in the reference department of public libraries. Reference desk librarians are usually eager to help you. After all, that is how they gain fulfillment and satisfaction from their job. One in particular, I recall, keeps a sign on her desk that says, "Disturb me a little . . . or a lot."

Mail List Brokers

Mail list brokers are good people to know. Their professional expertise has to do with who people are and where to find them.

Computers and word processors have vastly changed the state of the art of compiling and maintaining lists. If you have data processing equipment available, you may be able to purchase tapes of prospect lists ready to go. With sophisticated programming, lists can be merged or purged to further narrow them to a precise qualification. Here is where a specific profile of your best customer is most helpful. The computer can be programmed to retrieve only names matching your profile.

If you don't have data processing available, a good mail marketing firm can keep you up to date with the state of the art. Trade publications of the direct mail business such as *Direct Mail Marketing* and *Zip* make interesting reading and offer many tips. Never mind that you may not be in the direct mail business. The professionals in that business are masters at compiling and maintaining prospect lists. You can learn much from their experience.

Everybody Is a Source of Leads

Your acquaintances can provide you with good leads. Everyone you know or contact in any way, especially people who consider you their customer, are lead generators. Let them know what business you are in and that you are looking for business. Every chance you get, ask the question: "Who do you know that is looking for a good buy in [your product]?"

Occasionally in my seminars when I discuss the idea of getting leads from friends or business contacts, sometimes called *radiation,* one or two people in my audience say that they would be hesitant to do that because it would be taking advantage of a friendship or other connection. My stock answer to that is, "Does your auto mechanic feel embarrassed talking about fixing cars?" "Does your clothier hesitate to talk about fashions?" It usually makes the point.

Be active in trade or professional associations, service organizations, and community projects. The more active the better. Get involved. Be willing and eager to do favors for people. Noncompeting salespeople calling on the same clientele are excellent sources. Cultivate their friendship. Form networks with salespeople in your business in other parts of the country and exchange information. For my clients who have national distribution, I suggest a "Help

Each Other Memo," which is a standard form for salespeople in different parts of the country and the world to share lead information.

When making a call on a business firm, you often sit in the reception lobby for a while waiting until the person you are calling on is ready to see you. Most likely there are trade publications, house organs, company directories, and annual reports available especially for waiting visitors. Such publications are loaded with prime prospecting information. Here is an opportunity to turn otherwise unproductive time into profitable prospecting time.

Fairs and Trade Shows

Fairs and trade shows offer a unique opportunity to get leads, qualify prospects, and even close sales. A survey by the Trade Show Bureau determined that 57 percent of trade show attendees are looking for new products and services. It's a safe bet that most of the rest are at least looking for a chance to learn about what is new in their field of interest. They are top-level decision makers who buy or whose recommendations are respected. Besides, they are not as preoccupied with other matters as they might be on a typical sales call. You just can't beat that for opportunity, but it requires alertness to fully capitalize on it.

I am often a guest speaker or seminar presenter at a trade convention. I make a special effort to spend some time on the exhibit floor to learn more about my clients' business. It's a great source of ideas that enables me to customize my presentation for the specific concerns of the audience.

In some booths I see attendants enthusiastically engaged in conversation with delegates, making things happen. Others sit quietly, sometimes even looking bored and expecting passers-by to initiate a conversation or at least pick up some literature.

One of the smartest operators I ever saw was Bob Komasinski. He would ask each passer-by a simple five-word qualifying question that immediately told him whether or not he had a good prospect. It was a concrete industry convention. Bob sells equipment used by manufacturers of ready-mix concrete. The question was, "How much do you pour?" The more concrete they poured, the more equipment they used, and the more Bob was able to sell them.

The first time I walked past Bob I replied, "I don't pour concrete but I pour words out of my mouth. I'm the keynote speaker tomorrow morning." Bob smiled, introduced himself and said, "Hey, I'll be there listening." Then he turned his attention to the person walking behind me and asked, "How much do you pour?"

Later on I had a chance to chat with Bob away from his booth and complimented him on his heads-up technique. Bob said:

> I love conventions. I love people. I wish I could meet everybody here and get to know them better. There is a kind of carnival atmosphere to that exhibit floor that I have to separate my head from. It takes a certain amount of mental conditioning and discipline for me to do that. I'm not here just for the fun and excitement. This is a working day for me. One of the most important of the year. I'm here to sell that equipment. I just hope people passing my booth who are not prospects understand that and are not offended if I'm a little quick with them.

Yes, Bob Komasinski is right. Selling at trade shows is not for fun seekers or for timid souls. It can be an exhausting 16-hour day. Hangovers and lack of sleep can ruin one of the best selling days of the year.

You can increase traffic to your booth if you do some preshow promotion. Get a list of advance registrants from the show producers. Send them a letter or promotion piece offering a free gift, an idea, or some particular reason to visit your booth. Like Bob Komasinski, be ready with effective qualifying questions to identify your best prospects. Above all, take the initiative to meet attendees. Your best prospects will walk right past your booth if you let them.

Always Be Looking

In addition to all the above-mentioned sources of finding prospects, be sure to include just plain observation. In days gone by this was known as *smokestacking*. For those who sold to industry, where there was a smokestack, there was potential business. Today, the smokestack may well be replaced by a modern office building, but the concept of smokestacking, which simply meant being observant, is still sound. The outward appearance—of a building, a name on the door—may be a "smokestack" for you. Look for any new piece of construction, an unfamiliar sign on a building, or remodeling in progress. Don't drive by and wonder. Step in and find out! An early call on the occupant may give you a jump on competitors. Perhaps the occupant is new to the area. This gives you an opportunity to build early goodwill by offering to help with information based on your familiarity with the locale.

Concentrated Areas

It's a good idea to occasionally take alternative routes on your way to established customers to see whether anything new is going on in your territory. New office buildings are constantly going up, some in newly developed outlying areas. Industrial parks located near limited access highways are often growing and changing. They are easily reached and provide a concentration of prospects if you sell to a variety of businesses. They are especially good places to work early in the morning and late in the afternoon, when traffic clogs the main roads in a metropolitan area.

Many people who I knew were unsuccessful in their attempt to establish a career in selling thought that it didn't pay to make prospect calls before 9:30 in the morning or after 3:30 P.M., because traffic makes it impossible to get around. It always amazed me why it didn't occur to them to use that time of the day in a concentrated area off the beaten track or in a downtown area where they could park the car and walk. Perhaps they really wanted to fail.

Another advantage to working a concentrated area is that it is an easy and quick way to get the kind of qualifying precall information that separates suspects from prospects. Whenever you make a call, whether an established customer or prospect call, ask questions about other tenants in the vicinity. Often receptionists are good sources. They are accustomed to giving information to strangers, and if they've been at that location for any length of time, they are familiar with the neighborhood.

Keep Good Records

It is important to have a convenient method of filing and retrieving prospect information. Computers are great, but even if you have access to data processing you need some method to record information as you gather it and carry it with you as you move about the territory. Make it a habit to write down information as soon as you get it, preferably on the same form you use when making calls. Unless you need to record a lot of detail information, 3 × 5 or 4 × 6 cards are best. They are easily filed and carried on your person. By developing your own abbreviation code you can store a surprising amount of information on them.

A geographical file is most helpful. Whenever you plan to work a certain area, take the entire file of prospects for that locality. Even though your plans may be to work by appointment, if there is any open time, you can put it to profitable use by making some prospect calls in that locality after consulting your geographical file. This way your prime selling time will be booked solidly, thus giving you many opportunities to put business on the books that may have been otherwise missed.

Get Full Territory Coverage

In my consulting experience, as I conduct needs analysis studies for clients, I find there is a common need to train salespeople to get maximum coverage of their territories. Too often they are merely high-spotting the prospects who are easy to find. That's OK for the type of direct sales in which almost anybody can be a prospect, but getting only a fraction of the potential business out of a territory with limited clientele makes one a liability to oneself and to the company. It is interesting how often a new salesperson will take over a territory and immediately begin to double the previous business. Most of the additional business comes from prospects who were not being called on. The new salesperson does a more thorough job of prospecting.

Remember Gary Flaherty, who credited his success to the fact that he spent a good deal of time thinking about prospects. High on your "get done" list include adding a specific number of new prospects. You can't sell them if you don't know who they are.

5

How to Get Prospects to Want to See You

The Secret of Success

A young man went to see the wise man on the hill to find out the secret of success.

"Go over to the window, look out, and tell me what you see," the wise man told him.

"I see the marketplace," the youth replied.

"Now go look into the mirror over there and tell me what you see."

"Well, naturally, I see myself."

"In each case you were looking through a pane of glass. Tell me, what is the difference?" the wise man asked.

"The window is a clear pane of glass that allows me to see out and see the people in the marketplace. The mirror has a backing of silver that reflects my image."

"Ah, son. Therein lies the secret of success: when you let silver come between you and the people in the marketplace, you are going to see only yourself."

The marketplace is full of people with all kinds of problems—with all kinds of needs. They especially need counsel, guidance, and professional expertise in finding solutions to problems of vital interest to them and in making choices to fulfill their needs.

The world is full of organizations vitally interested in ideas that will help them to function more effectively, assure their survival, help them keep pace with the rapidly changing times, increase productivity, make more profit, cut costs, improve morale, improve internal communications, reduce accidents, avoid legal problems, satisfy customers, avoid losing key employees, avoid wasted effort. Individuals are vitally interested in ways to gain recognition, make more effective use of time, get more enjoyment out of life, improve their financial situation; to avoid mistakes, criticism, ridicule, fear, illness, death, pain, worry, or any one or combination of an unlimited number of concerns that are begging, sometimes silently, for solution.

To be sure, these concerns provide unlimited potential opportunities for salespeople all over the world. But before a transition can be made from potential to real opportunity, the right to be a provider of solutions must first be gained. This is most readily done when we put away our own personal concerns, forget what's in it for us when we make a call, and concentrate on what's in it for them—when we look out the window and see the people in the marketplace instead of looking in the mirror and seeing ourselves. This may sound idealistic to some, but there are compelling reasons why it is just downright practical.

What Is Meant by Maturity

In his book *The Mature Mind,* Harry Overstreet defines maturity as growing out of the self-contained ego—growing out of being self-centered and growing into becoming other-centered. We must not be very mature by Harry Overstreet's definition because psychologists tell us that we spend 95 percent of our time thinking about ourselves, about our own problems. Just stop and compare your untiring interest in what is happening in your own private world with your lack of concern about what is going on in the private world of almost everybody else. Realize that nearly everyone else alive is doing the same.

The Key to Motivation

To be effective in influencing and persuading others, we must be especially aware of this natural human tendency and make a conscious, deliberate effort to reverse this tendency. Because *people do things for their reasons, not ours*. Yes, that is a basic tenet of sales psychology. Presumably, this is well known even by those who have had the least amount of sales training. But years of observing salespeople in action makes me doubt if it is fully understood. I'm convinced there is no end to the depth of insight salespeople can get in that fundamental idea. The very fact that the natural human tendency to self-concern is so strong makes it imperative that the effort to counteract it be extraordinary.

Your Goals and Theirs

Chapter 3 dealt with the importance to a salesperson of setting goals, especially to get new business. But goals tend to be selfish. Your goals express what you want to achieve. Prospects have a different set of goals. For sure, they don't care much about yours. This is especially true when you are a total stranger.

What do you think of this as an opening remark from a salesperson on a call? "Mr. Prospect, my company is in business to make a profit, and if you buy some of our products, it will help us to reach our profit objectives for this year."

Ridiculous, isn't it? You would never say that. But often salespeople say something like that nonverbally with their manner, with an outward expression of an inner concern. Communications experts have been telling us for years that the overwhelming effect of communication is nonverbal. It's not the words but the feelings that are being transmitted. Ralph Waldo Emerson put it eloquently when he said, "Your actions speak so loudly, I can't hear what you say to the contrary."

To say this is not to diminish the importance of goal setting. In selling, goals must be confined to the planning stages, which include writing call objectives. But when you are in contact with prospects, their goals take number one priority. The only way you can satisfy your goals is to satisfy theirs.

Prospects or Opponents?

A mistaken impression persists among people today that a topnotch salesperson is a suave, dynamic persuader like the mythical one who could sell refrigerators to Eskimos. Along with this myth the notion persists that unless you're born with a super-dynamic magnetism, you're never going to make it to the top in selling. Now that may have been true years ago in some less informed, less sophisticated era. But it certainly isn't true today. People are constantly being bombarded with sales pitches on television and through other media. Today, they are more knowledgeable, more alert, more sophisticated, more wary. What happens when you're approached by a suave, dynamic persuader? How do you feel? You're ready to lock the safe, hide the checkbook; all kinds of defenses and smokescreens go up.

Then there is a fallacy that persists among some salespeople who see selling as a contest. If a sale is made, the salesperson wins and the customer loses. The language of selling often sounds like a strategy for a boxing match. To make points in a presentation is to "hit 'em with this." Dialog with the prospect is called sparring. Response to resistance is commonly called overcoming objections, and closing a sale is often referred to as delivering the knockout punch.

Prospects just don't want to be hit with unanswerable logic. They don't want to participate in a sparring match, much less be overcome and finally knocked out. People are like mirrors. They will reflect back to you your feelings toward them. If you see them as an enemy to be conquered, they will respond as the enemy putting up a defense, and their defensive position is a strong one. If you see them as a friend, they will return the friendship.

It's Easier to Be for Real

What is meant by reflecting feelings is much more than any external appearance or physical demeanor such as a friendly smile or a warm handshake. Smiles and handshakes are important! The friendlier and warmer, the better. But the underlying, deep-down, genuine feeling of warmth and friendliness must be there in order for the outward appearances to ring true. People today are more adept than ever before at detecting pretenders. They sense the tension between what is actually going on inside you and any mask you may choose to wear.

It is true, as Harvard psychologist William James declared around the turn of the century, that feeling follows action. That is, if you act a certain way, the feeling that goes with that action will come over you, as in the familiar platitude, "To be enthusiastic, act enthusiastic."

The exception to William James's dictum is commonly found in pretense. A parallel has often been drawn between selling and acting, even by champions of the sales profession. The salesperson is "on stage," face to face with a prospect and "acting out" the presentation. This kind of dramatics can be effective in a selling situation only if the n being acted out is in complete harmony with the real feelings going on inside the actor/salesperson. Otherwise it is a turnoff.

Hotshot Charlie Gets Burned

Let's follow a computer sales rep, we'll call him Charlie Smith, on a call to Joe Johnson, president of the Gopher Company. On the way over to the appointment, Charlie chuckles to himself as he plans his approach: "Mr. Johnson ought to be a pushover. He'd probably go-fer anything, ha ha! I'll hit him with our new model 101. I'll make his eyes pop out when I show him the revolutionary, super X feature. Then he'll knuckle under when he sees the complete software package. And I'll save our special finance plan for the coup de grace."

One thing about Charlie, he is positive. Another thing, he is enthusiastic. That's all fine, but the problem is with the third thing—he is ready to do battle. The adrenaline is pumping in the same way it was when Charlie played left tackle in college and there was an enemy on the other side of the scrimmage line. If the third thing isn't enough to be Charlie's undoing, then the fourth is. That is, Charlie is already planning how he's going to spend his commission check on this sale. Besides, this sale will put him in a special bonus bracket and that will make him enough money to afford the trip to Hawaii next January that he's been dreaming about. Just by coincidence, Charlie's car radio is playing Hawaiian music as he pulls into the Gopher Company parking lot.

Charlie greets Joe Johnson with a big smile and a hearty handshake, but Joe also sees the dollar signs in Charlie's eyes. Charlie is putting on an act for his own benefit, not Joe's, and Joe knows it. The coup de grace falls on Charlie when he wins an argument in logic, but loses the opportunity to make a sale.

Selling is not a contest. It is not a situation where one party wins and the other loses. Both can win. A prospect isn't someone to be tricked, manipulated, or dazzled with a phony act.

The Ideal Selling Situation

Bill Umphress of Chicago, who worked with me years ago selling sales training services, described the ideal selling situation in this way:

> Think of it as two old friends sitting down to discuss a mutual problem. Imagine the prospect is the guy next door who came to you for advice because you have had experience working with a problem situation he was facing.

Fred Hawkins sells industrial supplies for a distributing firm that maintains an inventory from many different manufacturers. By whatever yardstick you may choose to use, Fred is successful. His income from commissions and bonuses is higher than the total income of many of the top-level executives of manufacturers he represents. He thoroughly enjoys his work. Rarely does a month go by without Fred getting recognition for sales achievement in some manufacturer's bulletin. Fred and his wife love to talk about the expense-paid trips he has won to scores of the most fabulous resort spas of the world. Whenever Fred makes a sales call, the red carpet is rolled out to greet him. Here is what a plant manager of one of Fred's accounts has to say about him:

> I've asked Fred to call me first whenever he plans to come to my plant. Either I personally take him around to the people he should see or I make appointments for him with department heads, process engineers, or whoever may be involved in a purchasing decision. Fred is a walking reference manual regarding many of the tools and supplies we use. Not just what's what

but how best to use them. I have a shop coat for him hanging in my office closet. He wears it nearly every time he's here shoulder to shoulder with people on the shop floor. It's like having a specialist on my staff but he doesn't cost me a cent in payroll or fringe benefits except that I've instructed my people to never let Fred pick up a lunch check.

Fred is the exact opposite of the stereotypical, extroverted, dynamic persuader. Rather, he is a quiet, low-key kind of person. Fred told me:

I'll never forget those first few weeks when I started selling years ago. Talk about panic city. One call in particular, my hands were shaking so much I couldn't get the briefcase opened. Embarrassing! I was absolutely mortified. My mind must have gone blank because I don't even remember how I got out of there. Next thing I recall was driving to my next appointment in a cold sweat. This call was on a fairly small manufacturing plant. When I got there I just sat behind the wheel of my car feeling sorry for myself, wishing I had a nice comfortable job where I could work all by myself.

As luck had it, my negative train of thought was distracted when I noticed a truck being loaded at the rear door of the plant. The truck belonged to a machine shop a few blocks away that was also on my prospect list, but was not buying from us. What struck me as odd was that the pieces being loaded on the truck were unfinished components. I guessed these parts were being sent out to the job shop for machining operations this plant couldn't handle. The truck driver confirmed my suspicions. He further told me exactly what the machining operations were, how many trips he made back and forth each week, and how many pieces were loaded each trip.

Whatever self-pity or fear I had been experiencing quickly evaporated. I recalled that one of our suppliers had just sent us a brochure on a new attachment to a standard machine tool that would be able to handle this job. I suddenly saw my role in a different light. That company really needed me. I had an idea that was going to save them a lot of money. They were going to be glad I chose to call on them that day and that I chanced to park my car where I could see that truck being loaded. I wasn't just another salesman interrupting someone busy with other matters. I had something to show them that was so important, they had just better drop what they were doing and hear me out! I practically ran to the reception desk. I don't even remember what I said to the receptionist but it must have been pretty good because I recall the urgency with which she tracked down Mr. Schaefer, president of the company. When I sat down in his office this time, any fumbling with the briefcase was due to sheer excitement, not fear.

Yes, Mr. Schaefer bought my idea. Although he never was a big account in terms of volume, his business grew over the years and I don't believe he ever bought a product that we carry from any other source.

The most important sale I made that day was to myself when I sold myself on what my job is all about. From that time on I realized there must be hundreds of places in my territory that could improve their procedures in some way, who were using obsolete equipment and inefficient methods that were costing them time, dollars, waste, customer satisfaction, frustration, you name it. And my job was to look for those situations and show them a better way. I didn't see myself as someone selling products, I'm more like a consultant. The products got sold as a result of showing a better way.

Fred Hawkins has never lost his excitment for what he is doing and he doesn't have to put on a phony act to show it, for it is genuine. His enthusiasm is such a transparently sincere and honest emotion that it elicits trust and an equally sincere and honest consideration of his recommendations. It isn't something that Fred just turns on when he is in contact with customers.

Fred is a consummate student of the business. He reads everything he can get his hands on pertaining to the use of his products. He has antennas out, constantly scanning the world he travels in for new ideas and innovations. His world is beyond the office of purchasing agents where his competitors struggle with trying to "overcome objections," unaware of the real reason they are not getting any business. His world is out among the people who are using his products, where buying decisions are actually made. He wants to see what is going on, and he's constantly asking questions, learning and looking for ways to do it better. It's not that he snubs purchasing agents. He actually makes their job easier. He goes where he goes because his customers want him to be there.

Fred rarely has to ask for referrals. Names of prospects are given to him freely. Most often a customer will personally call the prospect and enthusiastically pave the way for him. When Fred does make an unsolicited call, he doesn't have to use any techniques. He just does what comes naturally. The excitement, the urgency, and the credibility surge forth from his reservoir of knowledge and experience.

Become an Expert

In subsequent chapters you will learn specific words, phrases, and techniques that will enable you to open the door and present your sales story to the proper buying authority on the most advantageous basis. The door-opening words, phrases, and techniques will be effective only to the degree that you understand and put into practice the concepts in this and the next chapter.

It is imperative that you see yourself as a competent, knowledgeable expert in your field and that you have information and ideas that will be of benefit to your prospects. This is a key point. Not only the product you sell, but you personally, by your interchange, will be of benefit to them. If you are new to the job, at least you have access to expertise through the resources in your company. You must furthermore make every effort to, in fact, become a competent, knowledgeable expert. Fred Hawkins did in his first few weeks on the job by being alert and observant.

After all, you are calling every day on people concerned with the same kind of problems. You have an exceptional opportunity to gather all the up-to-date information on the state of the art and trends in your industry. You are like a reporter who observes other people in action. You see different ones using your products and similar products in ways that bring them greater or lesser advantage. You see what works and what doesn't work. You are in a unique position to render valuable, practical expertise. Business firms, institutions, and government units willingly pay high fees to professional consultants for the kind of counsel you can offer free of charge. It is important to incorporate that dimension into the way you see yourself on your job.

Something Inside You Is Listening

Salespeople often call themselves peddlers. Of course, the term is typically used flippantly or in jest. But I believe there is something deep inside of us that doesn't realize it is being used in jest. Then our validity, our credibility, is tilted away from that delicate balance that often hangs in a prospect's mind as the decision is being made whether or not to grant an interview.

Before making a call, check your inner dialog. Ask yourself if you are going there to help someone solve a problem or to use someone to help solve yours. In your self-talk use positive, uplifting words to describe your role, such as problem finder, problem solver, consultant, idea giver, helper. Avoid words that suggest conflict—don't refer to your selling points as something to "hit 'em with," your precall planning as preparation for the attack, sales tools as weapons in your arsenal to overcome objections, and closing the sale as a victory.

For centuries philosophers have extolled the blessing of positive affirmations. Often their advice has been ridiculed by skeptics, but modern psychology has left no doubt the philosophers were right. Remember the quote by Dr. Albert Ellis in Chapter 2: "One has enormous control over one's emotions if one chooses to work at controlling them and to practice saying the right kind of sentences to oneself."

We are saying both positive and negative sentences to ourselves most of our waking hours, whether we are aware of it or not. A good way to practice saying the right kind of sentences, Dr. Ellis recommends, is to make a habit of repeating selected positive affirmations several times every day. Affirmations are most effective when you compose your own. The words you choose will reflect and bring into reality the kind of person you wish to become. Here is an example:

I am a confident, competent professional with special knowledge in the field of _____. My purpose in this profession is to help my customers to be more effective in manufacturing and marketing their products, so that they in turn can better serve their customers and provide opportunities for their employees. I enjoy my work and will be guided to say and do things that will contribute to my continued personal growth.

As you continue your personal growth in becoming more confident, competent, and knowledgeable in your field, and as you percieve the importance of that kind of growth more deeply, the people you call on will recognize your competence also. There will be no need for pretense or phony dramatics. Nor will you be handicapped with unnecessary stress caused by the burden of maintaining a contrived or combative posture. You can relax and just be yourself and let that natural personality do the job for you. Selling will become easier, more enjoyable, and more productive.

6

What People Want
to Buy

Jean Miller bought a new sewing machine. Her husband, Todd, bought a set of deadbolt locks for the exterior doors of their home.

Pat O'Neill, vice-president of sales of an insurance company, spent $20,000 for a sales incentive program.

Chester Kramer, resident of Pleasant Valley, bought a bag of the most expensive grass seed from his local garden store.

The Miller house is getting cluttered now that their four children are all teenagers. Jean really didn't want a sewing machine. It's just one more item to find room for. But the cost of buying ready-to-wear clothes for a family of six is more than the Millers' budget can stand. Besides, Jean really enjoys sewing. She bought cost reduction and pleasure.

Todd Miller didn't want any deadbolt locks. They are a bother to install and operate. But there have been several burglaries in the neighborhood recently. Todd bought security.

It was a struggle for Pat O'Neill to get budget approval for the incentive program. Several people on the executive committee didn't feel the company should be a Santa Claus to the agency force. Pat finally convinced them that profits from an expected sales increase would justify the expense.

No one, Chester Kramer included, wants seeds. Well, maybe birds do but they are not persons. Chester wants to have the greenest, thickest lawn on his block. He just loves to listen to compliments and he gets plenty regarding his beautiful lawn.

In Chapter 5 we reviewed a basic tenet of sales psychology: People do things for their reasons, not the salesperson's. Now we're going to take a close look at just what their reasons are and how you can translate what you sell into those reasons.

How to Get on the Buyer's Wavelength

What you may want to sell and what your customers want to buy are usually two different things. People don't buy anything for what it is. They buy what it will do for them. Too often sales opportunities are fumbled by a salesperson talking about the features of a product before the potential buyer understands the benefits. It goes unexpressed, but the buyer is thinking along these lines: "I don't care how good your goods are until you tell me how good your goods will make me."

On my desk is a case for my eyeglasses. It has a clip that fastens to my inside coat pocket. I don't give a darn about that clip except for what it does for me. And do you know what that little clip does for me? Clipped to my inside coat pocket, the case just plain feels better there. It feels better clipped securely to the pocket instead of bouncing around loose at the bottom. Another thing I like about the clip is that when the case is clamped to my inside pocket it looks better, keeps the coat looking neat instead of showing a big lump. Feels better, looks better. That's what I like about the clip. Another thing, I'm less likely to lose my glasses. With the high cost of eyeglasses, that's going to save me some money. One more thing about the clip: I once took my coat off in the men's room and guess where the eyeglasses fell. You probably guessed right.

The eyeglass case is made out of genuine leather. Now I don't give a darn about that except for what it does for me. And do you know what it does for me? I once had an inexpensive plastic case. After a few months' use it was so dog-eared, I was embarrassed every time I took it out. The leather one has been in use for years. It looks just as good as new. It doesn't embarrass me.

You can talk about clips. Talk about what they are made of, about the finest imported spring steel. But all that doesn't mean a thing to me until I understand that clipping my glasses case to my pocket feels better, looks better, saves me money, and keeps my glasses from falling someplace where they could get messy. You could tick off all the great things about leather and that doesn't mean a thing unless I know that I won't be embarrassed by it and that it's going to save me money in the long run because it's not going to wear out.

The clip and the fact that the case is leather are features. Feel better, look better, save money, avoid embarrassment, avoid a mess are benefits. Benefits refer to people, not to products. Benefits refer to all the human satisfactions a person will enjoy from using the product. Any details that describe the product usually are not benefits.

This doesn't mean you shouldn't talk about the features of your product. In fact, with many of the technical kinds of things being sold, more words in a sales presentation may need to be devoted to talking about features, facts, and specifics. But the features, facts, and specifics are going to be of little interest to a buyer until the benefits are clearly in mind. The features simply prove that the benefits do in fact exist.

Just like my eyeglass case. I don't care about the clip, or how it's made, or what it's made of until I'm aware of the human satisfactions I will get from those features. Please take special notice of the phrase *until I'm aware of the human satisfactions I will get*. This is a critical point. For benefits are always in the buyer's mind, never in the product.

Imagine that all the people you call on are wearing hats. And the hats have a big sign with the words, "So what?" Every time you mention your product or a feature of your product you must answer the question, "So what?" The answer to the "so what" question is a benefit.

How to Determine Buying Motives

Behavioral scientists give us a profound insight to make it easier for us to answer the "so what" question, to better understand the human satisfactions that motivate people to buy. It is this: *All human behavior can be traced to a person's desire for a feeling of well-being.* If people don't have a feeling of well-being, they will want to find it. Or if they have a little of it, they will want to increase it. If they already have the feeling of well-being, they'll want to avoid losing it. Or they will want to avoid the opposite depressed feeling. Associated with these feelings of well-being are four primary motives that are the reasons behind almost everything that has ever been bought.

The first of these is: *pride*. People want to gain or increase their feelings of pride. They want to own, use, and do things that will enhance their reputation and position. When you build a picture in a buyer's mind that offers recognition, approval, admiration, status, esteem, and ego satisfaction, you are selling benefits. Of course, you probably wouldn't use the words pride or ego satisfaction in your presentation. People don't like to admit those are important to them. You build a picture in their minds when you talk about an end result that they can identify in their world.

Suppose you were selling the grass seed to Chester Kramer. You might tell a story about another customer who bought that seed from you last year and how pleased he was when all of his neighbors raved about it.

On the other hand, people want to avoid criticism, ridicule, and disapproval. Consider how often you hear the expression, "What will the neighbors think?" That is fear of criticism. Or, "People must have thought I was nuts." That is fear of ridicule. These are powerful motives. Many people go through life with no more purpose than to get by with the least amount of discredit. They figure they've had a pretty good day at work if they don't catch heck from their boss.

There are countless examples of how powerful the pride motive is. When you explore the underlying cases of war, of threats of wars and consequent arms races, of suicides, of betrayed friendships, of marriage failures and broken homes, of mental breakdown, of personal conflict, even of vengeful murder, pride will be high on the list.

Motive number two: People want to increase their feelings of *pleasure*, and avoid the opposite feeling of pain or discomfort. They will pay readily and well for things and services that make them more comfortable, that make their lives and their work easier, that free them from mental and physical discomfort or drudgery. You are talking about benefits when you show people how their lives can be more fun, more exciting, more interesting, or how you can help them do their jobs easier, faster, or better.

Motive number three: People want to buy things that will increase *profit* or will help them avoid losses. This is a big one. More professional selling is aimed at this motive than any other. If you sell at the wholesale level, always keep in mind the fact that retailers don't want to stock their shelves with a lot of merchandise, they just want to make a profit. They want to hear the cash registers buzz. Whenever your prospects are in business, it is important to make them feel that your major purpose in life is to help them make more profit or cut costs, or to help them get, hold, and satisfy customers.

The desire to avoid losses is also important to consider, as often this motivation is stronger than the one to gain a profit. For example, suppose someone called you up at three o'clock on a cold, rainy morning and said, "Hey, there's a man out on your front lawn with a fifty-dollar bill. All you have to do is go out there and he'll give it to you." Chances are you would slam the telephone back down, crawl back into bed mumbling about some kind of a nut out there. But suppose someone called you up at three o'clock on a cold, rainy morning and said, "Hey, there's someone out on your front lawn carrying away that chaise lounge you just spent fifty bucks for." Chances are you would want to throw on a pair of jeans and a raincoat and go out there and try to stop him, wouldn't you? And that is true of most people. They are more strongly motivated to avoid losing what they already have than to gain a profit.

The fourth motive is: People want to buy what will increase their feelings of *security* or what will help them avoid anything that causes fear or anxiety. This covers things like safety, peace of mind, health, and self-preservation. Companies maintain purchasing departments to buy all kinds of goods and services to keep their business secure. Under security motives, buyers often have unspoken questions on their minds, such as: "Is it safe to buy from this person?" or "How can I be sure what I hear is true?" Put yourself in the buyer's place. Think of all the fears he may have and how you can help him to avoid those fears.

How Motives Relate to Each Other

You may have seen longer lists of motives. For example, how about food, clothing, and shelter? Ordinarily, these needs would be considered under security. But in our society today, food is more often bought for the pleasure it gives. Clothing is bought for pride. Shelter can be purchased for any one or combination of all four basic motives. Likewise, a person may gain a great deal of pleasure from making a profit and that also satisfies pride and security needs. So motives can be overlapping. Sex attraction is a powerful motive related to all four motives. Profit? Why yes, the cosmetics industry does pretty well appealing to that motive. Did you ever see anyone in a cosmetics ad in a magazine or on TV who didn't look prosperous?

The Essence of Selling

It doesn't matter that the product you sell or your business may be different from that of other salespeople. The people that you sell to are pretty much the same with the same basic human needs, wanting the same basic benefits. Virtually every human being you come into contact with will be stimulated into buying, or even just listening to your presentation, by these same basic motives. Truly these represent the real reason why almost any purchase is ever made.

Over the years I've heard many rhetorical discussions about the difference between selling tangibles and selling intangibles.

It is true that tangible products can be directly perceived by the senses—you can usually see them or see pictures of them, often touch them, perhaps even hear, taste, or smell them. But the sensory perceptions themselves are intangible, just as the reasons why people buy things are intangible.

Tangible products must ultimately be translated into intangible buying motives. To this extent all selling, whether of tangible products or intangible services, is much the same.

For the sake of simplicity in this book I will refer to what is being sold as a product. If you sell a service or other intangible, I trust you will have no problem relating to the word *product*.

So then, what you have to sell in your product or service is not its features, or its function, or its price, or its quality, or its size or volume or shape or color. Selling, in its purest sense, is simply translating all that factual information into the benefits that serve the prospect's self-interest whether it be pride, pleasure, profit, or security. That is not to say you must use all four of those appeals every time. Often just one may be the most important concern of a particular prospect. In that case you need only concentrate on that one. For example, if you sell to business firms, you can be pretty sure they want to make more profit or cut costs. If you're not sure what the main buying motive is, a few timely questions can help you avoid making wrong assumptions. In subsequent chapters you will learn how to determine a prospect's dominant buying motive by using effective probing techniques. One wrong assumption you want to avoid, however, is that the people you approach will make the translation from product features to human satisfactions themselves.

How to Avoid a Fatal Assumption

Jerry Clement's point of view is typical of many salespeople I've met. Jerry was on the sales staff of a chemicals manufacturer client of mine. I was assigned to spend a day working with him as part of a training needs analysis I was preparing for the company. When making calls with salespeople during a needs analysis, I never coach or critique their performance. My task is strictly to ask questions and observe.

Jerry knows his products well. He prides himself on the fact that he could quote facts verbatim from the brochures and catalog sheets. Inasmuch as he knew I was in the sales training business, Jerry wanted to express his opinion of the company's past efforts in that department. "Last year at the annual sales meeting," Jerry recalled, "we spent three days role playing on explaining the benefits in the features of our products. You know, that all sounds good in theory but we can't really use that stuff on a call. Most of the people we call on have degrees in chemistry. They know what our products do. I'd feel foolish if I had to say all of those obvious things."

Now Jerry may be right in assuming that many of the people he calls on know what his products do. But Jerry is wrong if he assumes they will be thinking of those benefits when he comes to call.

Remember what was said earlier in this chapter—that benefits are in the mind of the buyer, not in the product. It follows, then, that *if the buyer is not thinking of benefits, the benefits don't even exist for that buyer at that time*. Features can exist without the prospect, but the benefits cannot.

Be mindful of this especially when making first-time calls on new prospects. If they are preoccupied with other matters, if they are wondering whether or not you are a time waster, if they are thinking they're satisfied with their present situation, or any one of numerous other ifs, it's a pretty safe assumption the benefits will not be in their minds unless you make a special effort to help them focus on benefits.

Never take for granted that the benefits are self-evident. The essence of the task of selling is to translate product features into benefits *in the mind* of the prospective buyer. In becoming properly familiar with a product, it is easy to lose sight of the fact that buyers just don't have the initial interest to spend time and effort making the translations for themselves. They may know what the benefits are, but if they are not thinking benefits, your efforts will be for naught. Even a low price by itself doesn't mean much. Only when a person is aware that the sum total of benefits is going to equal or exceed the price will that person be willing to pay the price. Likewise, only when a person is aware that the benefits of listening to your presentation are going to equal or exeed the value of the time spent will that person be willing to spend the time.

Simplify Your Approach

Perhaps in your previous sales training you learned of an intermediate element between a feature and a benefit known as an *advantage*. The idea here is you first convert a feature into an advantage before it is translated into a benefit. An advantage is usually defined as the way a feature is used to solve a problem. For example, if you were selling some kind of machine, you might say, "This machine has sealed bearings [feature], so it will never require oilings [advantage], and that will make your job easier [benefit]." I find this extra step causes confusion in the minds of many salespeople. I've listened to many useless discussions about whether something is an advantage or a benefit. The fine line between an advantage and a benefit is often blurred. There may be more reason to consider an advantage as an extra step in a detailed or technical presentation that allows time to make demonstrations which include advantages. But an introductory remark aimed at gaining the attention of a prospect needs to be shorter.

Better to keep it simple. Better to just keep clear in your mind the basic principle that people do things for their reasons, not yours. Better to spend your time and effort in discovering what those reasons are. Better to be thinking of ways to translate the features of what you sell into a combination of advantages and benefits to your prospects without mentally struggling with which is an advantage and which is a benefit. Whether advantages or benefits, both are in the buyer's interest.

Offer Plus Values

In addition to benefits directly related to features of your product give some thought to possible benefits unrelated to the product itself. These could be any service you have to offer, such as technical assistance, merchandising, co-op advertising, resale help, billing, financing, market research, delivery, or any other service that is unique to your business. Of course, also keep in mind the counsel, guidance, and useful ideas you can offer on the basis of your experience and know-how.

One of my clients is a mobile-home manufacturer. A problem its dealer organization faces, especially when interest rates are high, is financing the inventory on its sales lots. The manufacturer developed a superb audiovisual presentation that showed every model and every possible combination of interior design it makes. It even designed one of its models as a studio to show the presentation. The benefit to the dealer, unrelated to the product itself, was increased profits through opportunities to make more sales and at reduced inventory expense. Such extra benefits often will give you a competitive edge, especially when price competition may be a factor. Buyers become less concerned about price when benefits unrelated to the product itself offer plus values.

This Will Keep You on Track

Here is an idea to help you constantly reinforce the principles outlined in the last two chapters. Take several 3 × 5 cards and with a marking pen write this question on each card in large, bold letters: "WHAT DO I REALLY SELL?" Now attach one card to the sun visor of your car, put another in a prominent position on your desk, another inside your briefcase, and another in any other place where you will notice it as you go about your day. Then several times a day, especially just before a call on a prospect either in person or on the phone, answer that question to yourself in as many ways as you can think of without mentioning or describing the product you sell. Answer that question in terms of benefits to your customers, in terms of all the human satisfactions they will enjoy as a result of buying from you.

Your Self-Esteem will Soar!

You will put a lot more "sell" in your selling efforts when you consciously and deliberately think and talk about all the good things your product will do for prospects instead of what it is, about what's in it for them instead of what's in it for you, about benefits instead of features.

You will be more eager to make calls, as you will feel better about yourself and your job. You will no longer feel that prospects are doing you a favor by granting an audience, but rather that you are the one with favors to offer with profitable ideas, counsel, guidance, and professional expertise, in addition to the benefits to be gained from your product. For when your concern is truly for your prospects, your words will flow with a sincerity of purpose and natural enthusiasm that will be both captivating and convincing.

7

The Magic Door Opener

AIDA Revisited

Some years ago, before many of the active salespeople of today were even born, a simple sales technique was taught throughout the land known as the AIDA formula. AIDA is an acronym that identified four steps, in their proper sequence, necessary to make a sale. Using this formula, you first need to gain the *attention* of the prospect to listen to you. Next step is to create *interest* in what you have to say. Then you build a *desire* for what you have to sell, and finally you call for *action* that closes the sale.

The only problem with the AIDA formula, if there ever was one, was overexposure. After years of expounding it in books and training sessions it ultimately became old hat. It is interesting to note that the reasons, rooted in human nature, which made the AIDA formula effective never changed, because human nature hasn't changed. The only thing that changed was the attitudes of trainers, writers, and the salespeople being trained. Another side of human nature seems to propel us to abandon the wisdom of the ages and cause us to seek new, sophisticated, less commonplace wisdoms. The recent history of the organizational training movement is replete with fads that come and go. Actually, many of the newer fads are nothing but old hats with new ribbons.

Getting back to the AIDA formula, the reality is, that you're just not likely to close a sale unless you build desire on the part of prospects. Likewise you can't build desire until you gain interest, and that doesn't happen without getting their attention.

This Sale Comes First

The kind of closed sale we are primarily concerned with in this book is sometimes referred to as the *sale before the sale*, that is, the time spent building sufficient desire on the part of a prospect to agree to listen to your sales presentation. The time frame that contains all four steps of the AIDA process in opening situations is compressed into a matter of just a few minutes, sometimes even less than a minute. Therefore, you must come forth with the strongest attention and interest getter you can conceive in order to do the job quickly, not to overpower your prospects but rather appeal to their self-interest.

The Human Sparkplug That Ignites People to Action

To find a strong appeal, let's go back to the behavioral scientists, who gave us the important insight in Chapter 6 that *all human behavior can be traced to a person's desire for a feeling of well-being*. Please take special notice of the word *feeling*. Human behavior is determined by emotion much more than by logic.

Now consider what happens when someone does not have a feeling of well-being. Recall the times when you are deprived of good feelings. Think of being too cold or too hot, hungry, thirsty, tired, bored, or otherwise uncomfortable. The more discomfort you fell in any of these situations, the stronger will be your urge to do something to relieve the feeling of discomfort and return your feeling of well-being. In other words, the discomfort felt when a person is deprived of well-being or envisions possible loss of well-being is a powerful force that will propel that person to take action. This is important to consider when you want to gain the attention of someone who appears disinterested. The degree of interest will depend on the degree of relative dissatisfaction a person feels. Someone who feels satisfied will see no reason to change the present situation, and is therefore not interested in considering any action to cause it to change.

Suppose you feel fine, everything is going great. A friend says, "I've got this new headache remedy that just beats anything I've ever used." Your reaction is probably something like, "That's nice." It's just small talk. You would just as soon talk about something of livelier interest.

On the other hand, suppose you have a splitting headache. You would give almost anything to go home and go to bed but you have an appointment with your biggest customer, who is about to renew a contract. Tomorrow the customer leaves on a Caribbean cruise and you know that one of your competitors will be on that same ship. A friend says, "I've got this new headache remedy that just beats anything I've ever used." You bet you're going to be interested!

Consider a third situation. You are feeling fine. Everything is going great. A friend says, "Suppose you have a splitting headache. You would give almost anything to go home and go to bed but you have an appointment with your biggest customer, who is about to renew a contract. Tomorrow the customer leaves on a Caribbean cruise and you know that one of your competitors will be on that same ship. Well now, I've discovered a new headache remedy that just beats anything I've ever used. And if you ever had a headache in a situation in which you just had to keep going, it would really save the day for you."

Your interest in the third situation may not be quite as high as it was in the second situation but it will certainly be a lot higher than it was in the first one.

Feelings are only temporary. They can be changed. Success in gaining the attention of a prospect often hinges on your ability to bring about an awareness of a dissatisfaction. Just as benefits do not exist unless they are *in the mind* of the prospect, feelings connected with the loss of well-being do not exist unless that person is actually experiencing or envisions such loss.

An Attention-Getting Masterpiece

Remember Professor Harold Hill in the Broadway hit musical *The Music Man?* Professor Hill toured the country selling band instruments and band uniforms. He had a good grasp of the principle of making people aware of problems they didn't know they had. The day he arrived in River City he saw a pool table being moved into a building owned by the local mayor. That evening when the citizens of River City were milling around the town square. Professor Hill went into a song and dance called "Ya Got Trouble." Using many vivid images, he convinced the people that the moral character of their whole town—and especially of their children—would be seriously threatened by the new pool hall.

In a four-minute song, he used the word *trouble* 15 times. In chorus the townsfolk chanted the word *trouble* in the background over 80 times. How is that for getting attention? How is that for getting feedback from the prospects confirming their awareness of the problem?

Now everyone was keenly interested in hearing about a solution. And, of course, his solution was to have a boys' band. Their sons would be practicing every day after school instead of hanging around the pool hall. And wouldn't every mom be proud to see her son marching in a parade down Main Street in a fancy uniform and playing "Seventy-Six Trombones"?

Professor Harold Hill had a good grasp of the need to get people to envision the loss of feelings of well-being as an attention getter. He knew he didn't stand a chance of getting the folks interested in his merchandise until they first saw it as the remedy to big trouble.

Of course, Professor Hill was guilty of some exaggeration in dramatizing the trouble in River City. Perhaps it was done for the sake of adding an important piece of showmanship to a musical comedy. The example from *The Music Man* isn't used here to advocate dishonesty. Unfortunately, there are unscrupulous people who apply this principle to swindle others.

As I wrote this chapter, a local television news team was running an exposé of a basement waterproofing company that advertises for a free inspection of potentially leaking basements. Their "inspectors" are trained to tell *all* the prospects who respond to the ad that their basement walls are in danger of collapsing unless they are willing to spend several thousand dollars for a waterproofing job. You will find "furnace inspectors" who warn of defectless furnaces about to blow up and auto mechanics that sell unneeded repairs. I even remember a doctor who once pointed a warning finger at me as he said, "Get those tonsils before they get you!" Well, those tonsils are still in my throat many years later, thanks to another doctor who asserted that there clearly was no reason for them to be removed.

Yes, there are those who will tell lies to achieve selfish ends. Their shabby conduct need not restrain you from using truthfulness to help people become aware of real problems that stand in the way of a better life for them. The world is full of people with legitimate problems, people who need only honest and objective guidance to show them a better way.

You Don't Need a Song and Dance

The core insight in this River City example is the importance of bringing to the center of your prospects' attention a clear mental picture of a problem, getting them to agree that it is a problem, and getting them to realize that they are dissatisfied enough about it so that they want to consider how to resolve the problem.

Therein lies the magic door opener!

I like to use the phrase "trouble in River City" as a mnemonic device to remind me of what I need to do to get people's attention and spark their interest. I need to find their "trouble in River City" and talk about that first. I must be genuinely interested in their problem. At the attention-getting stage, what I have to sell is not even mentioned. It has no place in the conversation until their problem, their dissatisfaction is clearly in focus.

For example, follow me on a call on an executive of a company to sell a new sales training program. As often happens, I will spend some time in the reception lobby waiting until my prospect is ready to see me. Reception lobbies usually have magazines lying around and they present an opportunity to catch up on reading. I reach for one with a provocative headline on the front cover. But wait! My mnemonic device shifts into action. I remember that the important issue at hand is "trouble in River City." This company must have some problems. Their salespeople are probably missing some business in situations where they could be making sales. What are those situations? I look for company literature, brochures, catalogs. I ask the receptionist some questions about the products they sell. I try to relate all this new information with experiences I've had consulting with other companies in similar situations. When I finally get face to face with my prospect, my consciousness is totally involved with trying to find the "trouble in River City." It's the ideal mental state to slide right into my opening remark and then probe for the specific problem my prospect has. In Chapter 11 you will learn how to compose the exact wording of an effective opening statement. But for now we are primarily concerned about the ideal mental state to be in for an opener.

Of course, I have call objectives. Those objectives may include closing the sale. But my success in meeting the objectives is going to first depend on my ability to identify the problems this company may have and to get my prospect to think enough about them at this time to want to consider my solutions.

A Positive Approach

When I illustrate this point in my seminars, occasionally some participants question it. They wonder if putting all that emphasis on someone else's problem might be considered a negative approach. Perhaps you feel this way too. But the end result of our effort is a solution to the problem. What could be negative about that? If you agree that people do things for their reasons, putting their problems in clear perspective gets them to realize that you are genuinely concerned about their reasons.

You can begin by talking about all the wonderfully positive things about your product and you will sound like so many other salespeople who have dollar signs in their eyes. Your prospects won't be interested in solving that problem! It's just a fact of human nature that in order to get anyone interested enough to consider a solution, the problem must be clearly in focus first. No realization of a problem, no need to think about a solution.

Talk about aspirin would not be of much interest to people who feel good. But talk about aspirin when they have a headache, or envision the possibility of having one, brings about an entirely different level of interest. Recall the aspirin commercials on TV. They first show a person in pain, before aspirin comes into the picture.

Sellers Make a Better World

Besides, I don't believe dissatisfaction is negative. I believe it is one of the most powerfully positive, creative forces in existence. If our ancestors had not been dissatisfied we would still be living in caves, wondering where our next meal is coming from. Dissatisfaction has released us from the drudgery of all kinds of back-breaking toil. Its creative force has given us all of the marvelous labor-saving conveniences that allow us to use our energies for even more creative pursuits. Dissatisfaction has eradicated the fear and heart-break caused by diseases we don't even need to think about anymore such as polio, tuberculosis, smallpox, and diphtheria. It is going to find a cure for cancer, find a substitute for oil as an energy source, and even figure out a way for nations to live at peace with one another.

Dissatisfaction, negative? Not at all. We need more of it! And we need salespeople who are sowers of dissatisfaction. For if we have the highest standard of living in all human history, with an incredible volume and variety of comforts, luxury, convenience, and security, it is because in countless separate instances *somebody sold somebody something*.

Helping Prospects to Greater Satisfaction

Satisfaction and dissatisfaction are only states of mind. People often just think they are satisfied when in fact they are merely content to maintain the status quo. Remember Newton's First Law of Motion that states "any body in a state of rest will remain in a state of rest unless it is acted upon by some outside force." That's what selling is all about. It is the outside force that brings to light dissatisfaction with the status quo and moves people to enjoy greater satisfaction.

Think of the times you have approached prospects whose initial, knee-jerk reaction was "not interested," yet later at some point they bought from you. The need was present at the first contact but they simply were not aware of the need.

Most people are not completely satisfied at any given time. They don't have so much esteem, pleasure, profit, or security that they would not trade it for more esteem, more pleasure, more profit, or more security. To show the possibility of more satisfaction usually makes them dissatisfied with their present situation.

Turn a prospect's satisfaction into dissatisfaction by offering greater satisfaction.

8

Keeping Yourself Out of Trouble

Prince Dacun, the king's favorite son, lay dead on the battlefield. The young warrior Pion is given the swiftest horse to bring the message of the prince's death back to the king. All night in a driving rainstorm Pion rides through hostile territory, until the horse falls beneath him from exhaustion. At dawn he is captured by enemy soldiers and severely beaten. Since he is young and strong the soldiers decide to let him live and sell him as a slave. One night the soldiers drink too much wine and Pion makes his escape. On foot, traveling mostly at night in order to avoid capture, trudging over mountains, swimming through icy streams, fighting off wild animals, battered and exhausted, Pion finally makes it back to the palace to give the king the bad news. His reward? The king orders him beheaded!

This is an often used theme dating back to Greek mythology. It reveals something about human response to bad news. Surely an exaggerated response by present-day standards of civilization, but it suggests a note of caution when confronting people with their problems.

If you are the bearer of bad news, especially if the news implies criticism of your prospect's efforts, chances are you will find, not your head, but the relationship cut off. In other words you would be the one in trouble in River City. Does this sound like a catch-22? On the one hand, we need to make people aware of their dissatisfac-

tions, of their problems, of their needs. On the other hand, if we
bring up these matters we put the relationship in jeopardy. But
bring up these matters we must. Only we must do it tactfully.

How to Use Tact

The finest expression of tact in revealing your prospects' needs is
to allow them to state their needs in their own words. The word
allow is used here to make it clear that you subdue the temptation to
directly state the problem yourself even though it is obvious to you.
People respond to their own words and ideas with far greater
conviction than anyone else's. If they sense your words are based on
your self-interest the response is sure to be negative. The best way
to help people state their needs in their own words is through the
skillful use of questions. This is known as the indirect approach.

Preparing Questions for a Call

When I work with salespeople in the field, rarely do I see them
prepare questions in advance of a call. Even when they understand
that people do things for their own reasons, and understand the
difference between features and benefits and the importance of
emphasizing benefits, they still often make the mistake of immediately launching into a sales presentation based on what they think
should be of interest to the prospect, instead of finding out. They
plan the presentation in terms of what they are going to *tell* a
prospect but rarely plan the questions they will *ask*.

Remember the TV comic playing the part of an oriental seer who
can give answers before he knows the questions? If you try that
routine on a call, your prospects may not think it's very funny—or
relevant. The questions you ask can be more important than
anything you say. Prospects may not believe the statements you
make but they will certainly believe their own answers to the
questions being considered. Unless you possess the capability of
being adept at thinking on your feet, you will ask much more
purposeful questions when you take the time to plan them carefully
in advance.

And I do mean prepare them carefully. Often when the suggestion is made to salespeople that they prepare questions in advance, I observe this reaction, "Oh yes, let me see, I was supposed to think up some questions." Then there will be a hodgepodge of random questions for the sake of having some questions rather than questions designed to achieve a specific objective. This is another reason why call objectives are so important. If you know what you want to accomplish on a call, it is easier to design a game plan to accomplish your objective. Relevant questions are part of the game plan. Otherwise, you get the hodgepodge that only leads to frustration.

Questions Offer Many Benefits

Often when prospects say they're not interested, it doesn't necessarily mean that they're never going to be interested. It just means that at that time their minds are occupied with something else. But most people are conditioned to respond to questions and will when asked. Questions are an excellent way to break through this preoccupation barrier.

Skillful use of questions is the primary method of qualifying prospects—of determining if a suspect is a prospect. Answers to your questions and, sometimes more important, the manner in which they are answered give you clues to the priority each will be assigned and to the strategy you will use to convert these prospects into customers.

Asking questions affords an opportunity to get in tune with your prospects, to ascertain where they are emotionally and intellectually. You learn their language—words and phrases that are meaningful to them. Conversely, you will know what expressions may be unfamiliar to them and so avoid misunderstanding and the risk of being turned off.

Questions give prospects a greater sense of participation in an interview. People crave recognition. When used with skill, questions are an excellent form of giving recognition. With questions, you can make people feel important, that you respect their opinion.

Who Is Most Interesting?

In your own experience, who do you find to be the most interesting persons to talk with? Is it those who can captivate you with all the great things going on in their lives? Those who can dazzle you with all the wisdom they have on a variety of different subjects? Do you just sit and listen in amazement, utterly speechless? Or are you bored and somewhat peeved because you can't get a word in?

On the other hand, how do you feel about a person who asks questions about you, questions that take a benevolent tone of genuine interest in you and in what you feel free to reveal about yourself? Don't you find that kind of person a much more interesting partner in conversation?

Setting the Right Tone

This matter of tone is important, because questions asked for self-serving purposes can sound unfriendly, even threatening. Let's face it. There is a self-serving element in the salesperson's role. We set goals. We have call objectives that include making sales. Our livelihood, our jobs depend on that. We are held accountable if we don't. If we are not careful our self-interest will show through.

Questions can often raise doubts, make challenges, or imply disagreement with someone's point of view. Then too, remember the kind of questions parents and schoolteachers used to ask when your behavior and/or performance fell short of their preference.

> Where have you been?
> How many times do I have to tell you . . .?
> When are you going to shape up?
> Why did you do such a thing?

Stored in the recesses of everyone's memory are the feelings of guilt, humiliation, and lack of acceptance caused by such questions. You certainly want to avoid dredging up those feelings.

What Is Meant by Control

It is often said that questions should be used to control a sales interview. I believe *control* is an unfortunate choice of words. It carries with it connotations such as dominate, subdue, having it all one's way. This is exactly the opposite of what you want people to feel you are doing to them.

The other side of the control coin is a common notion on the part of salespeople that they "should be in control" of the sales interview, and that whenever they are not in control, they are demonstrating lack of competence.

This is an erroneous notion. If you ever have it, get rid of it. To believe you should be in control when you are not is going to trigger a downward emotional spiral. You will feel a twinge of anxiety in the pit of your stomach. This causes further loss of confidence. Then you lose some poise and, in fact, are not performing at your best. So now you've gone from a mental perception of lack of competence to the real thing. And it's needlessly self-imposed.

To me, this fallacy about a salesperson's compulsion to control a sales interview is a curious one. How absurd to think that you should be able to control a situation where the host is used to being in full control, and where you have a few minutes to start making sense before interest wanes and the host begins to look for ways to terminate the conversation. Who is going to be in control?

Initiative, I believe, is a better word than control. Asking questions is taking the initiative to establish the subject under discussion. Skillful use of questions keeps the discussion on track and provides the initiative to bring it back on track if it wanders in a different direction. Sometimes despite your best efforts it's going to wander beyond your ability to bring it back. Now if you've heard of legendary super salespeople who are able to control anybody every time, don't you believe it!

How to Eliminate the Prospect's Defensiveness

Selling has been characterized as an art in the sense that it is studied action and skilled execution in conducting a human activity. The essence of this skill is knowing and respecting the fine line between your and the prospect's goals. It is being effectively straightforward in asking purposeful questions that will allow you to apply your knowledge and experience in helping someone to identify a problem without putting that person on the defensive.

It will be helpful to get that fine line in focus if you examine your motives before planning questions to ask on a sales call. Are you trying to genuinely help someone find a better way? Or are you trying to be clever, to manipulate, to trick so you win, they lose? For if you do that, you are inviting defensiveness. You aren't going to help your own cause by putting prospects on the defensive.

The Kinds of Questions to Ask

You further lessen their defensiveness when you earn the right to ask questions. In the long term, you earn the right by becoming knowledgeable about your field. Remember the story of Fred Hawkins in Chapter 5. When Fred asks questions, his customers listen and are usually eager to answer because they recognize him as an expert who has valuable information to offer.

But on a more immediate basis, on a particular call, you earn the right to ask questions first by asking permission to ask some questions. Secondly, you reduce defensiveness by explaining why you are asking the questions. The reasons why, of course, are the prospect's reasons, not yours. For example:

> Mr. Prospect, based on our experience with other companies similar to yours, I believe we have some ideas that can lower your costs. But first I will need to know a few things about your operation so as not to make any wrong assumptions. Do you mind if I get your answers to a few questions?

> In the interest of conserving time, so we can quickly determine if my ideas have an application here, could I get your answers to a few questions?

Closed-End Questions

There are two types of questions you will want to consider using. Closed-end questions, sometimes called directive or fact-finding questions, are those that can be answered with a yes or no or simple statement of fact. Here are some examples of closed-end questions:

> How many people do you employ?
> Have you ever heard of our company?

What brand of product are you currently using?
When will you be receiving another shipment?
Who supervises this project?
Where is your head office located?
Does this sound reasonable to you?

Closed-end questions are important to gather factual information you need to know, to start a conversation, to gain the attention of someone preoccupied with other matters, to draw out someone who may be unwilling to talk, to change the direction of a conversation, to clarify a point, to check for degree of interest or understanding on the part of another person, and to confirm an agreement.

Open-End Questions

Open-end questions, sometimes called nondirective or feeling-finding questions, cannot be answered with a yes or no or a simple statement of fact. They must be explained at some length. Here are examples of open-end questions:

How does this affect your business?
What is it you like about Brand X?
What is it you don't like about Brand X?
What kind of comments do you get from your customers regarding this product?
How do you feel about this?
Why is that important to you?
What directions will you be taking in this regard?

Open-end questions allow people to feel a greater sense of participation in an interview. They give it a more conversational tone—more of the atmosphere of two old friends sitting down to discuss a mutual problem. Obviously, with a stranger you're not an old friend. But open-end questions bring you a little closer to that ideal relationship as quickly as possible.

In answering open-end questions your prospects are more likely to give you in-depth information that helps you to diagnose their needs—information you would not get from strictly closed-end questions. You gain not only factual information, but also a view of the all-important opinions, attitudes, and feelings which have so much bearing on their actions. It is in these off-the-cuff verbalizations that your prospects usually clarify their thinking, state their needs in their own words, or give you a clue for paraphrasing their statements if necessary, to further clarify an expression of need. Paraphrasing means repeating what someone said, but in different words. You will learn more about this technique in Chapter 16.

Turning Statements into Questions

Some statements can be turned into questions by tagging them with, "Isn't it?" or "Do you agree?" or "What has been your experience with that?" For example:

> This is a new marketing opportunity for you, isn't it?
> Many of our customers see an increasing demand for the bigger models. What has been your experience?

The Importance of Balance

In my seminars, I often have salespeople write out a list of questions they ask on three different categories of calls: (1) new prospects, (2) prospects called on before who are giving all or most of their business to a competitor, and (3) current customers. For several years I kept track of the kind of questions listed. Ninety-four percent were closed-end questions.

Of course, closed-end questions are important. They provide much needed factual information in addition to being useful for the other reasons stated earlier. But sales will be made easier and more often with judicious use of open-end questions.

When planning the questions you will ask on a particular call, be careful that you don't string too many closed-end questions in sequence. It can be a source of irritation for a person to answer a steady flow of closed-end questions. It can sound like some sort of unpleasant inquisition, such as a third degree or witness stand interrogation. How does this dialog between a hardware rep and a retail chain buyer sound?

Buyer: Do your stores carry metal-cutting drills larger than 3/8 inch?
Rep: Yes.
Buyer: How large do they go?

Rep:	One inch.
Buyer:	Do you handle star drills?
Rep:	No.
Buyer:	How about taps in sets?
Rep:	Yes.
Buyer:	Individual taps?
Rep:	Yes.
Buyer:	Metric sizes?
Rep:	Yes.

Compare that commentary with this one:

Rep: Can you tell me something about the kind of drills, taps, and star drills you carry?

Buyer: Why, yes. Many of our stores are in smaller towns in rural areas. Farmers need heavy-duty, industrial-quality tools. So we stock larger sizes than stores in cities catering to primarily the do-it-yourself trade. Besides the farmer, we also serve local industry as they usually don't have convenient access to an industrial supply firm. Here again, we carry a good supply of large sizes, metric sizes, and individual pieces for replacement purchases in addition to sets. You mentioned star drills. Our stores carry them but purchase of all concrete tools is handled by the paint purchasing department.

The first example was six closed-end questions. The second example was one open-end question that elicited a lot more valuable information in a much more congenial atmosphere.

Sometimes you may have to ask several closed-end questions to draw out the specific information you need. In such cases, break the sequence with an occasional open-end question to loosen up the dialog.

Changing the Style of Questions

A closed-end question can be turned into an open-end question by the way it is phrased. Here are some examples:

Closed:	Do you use word processing equipment?
Open:	To what extent do you use word processing equipment?
Closed:	Do you have any problems with that machine?
Open:	What is your experience with that machine?

Closed: Do you like to travel?
Open: How do you feel about traveling?

Some closed-end questions can be tagged with an open-end question simply by following up with "why?" or "why is that?" or "why is that important to you?"

How to Ask Why

Why is one of the most difficult questions for adults to ask. For the first few years after they learn to speak, little children don't seem to have any trouble with it. Later they learn that voices of authority, parents, teachers, bosses often get impatient when responding to a why. At times the answer comes out, "Because I said so, that's why!" They learn that to avoid arousing a negative emotion, they shouldn't ask why.

When you ask why, it is important not to imply any judgment such as criticism or disapproval of the other person's position. Often this kind of judgment shows up in your tone of voice, a raised eyebrow, a squint, a hand gesture. If these come across in a way that suggests you disagree, you will be sure to trigger defensiveness on the part of your prospect. These nonverbal signals just happen unconsciously.

Keep in mind your motives for asking questions. If it is to manipulate, to attack, to trip up a prospect for your reasons, then you will tend to reveal that nonverbally. But if you are in full realization of the number one priority as helping someone find a better way, you won't need to be concerned about your body language. Instead, you can concentrate on the matter at hand.

Here are some alternatives to why that have a softer sound:

> Obviously you have a good reason for saying that. Do you mind telling me what it is?
> What do you have in mind?
> How do you feel about this?
> How do you arrive at your decisions?
> What factors determine your decisions?
> If I knew what factors determine your decisions, I could be more specific. Could you tell me?

Could you elaborate on that?

Could you give me some examples?

Or simply ask for permission to ask why:

Do you mind telling me why?

Find the Feelings

Open-end questions are sometimes called feeling-finding questions. Inasmuch as people do things for emotional reasons, open-end questions open the door for exploring this critical decision-making emotional background. Using the word *feel* in questions can be more effective than using the word *think*. For example, you could ask, "What do you think about that?" Better to ask, "How do you feel about that?" It is easier for people to talk about how they feel than about how they think.

Your Own Motivation Research

Consumer advertising campaign approaches are sometimes based on in-depth motivation research. An important technique researchers use is what is known as testing the extremes—that is, finding out what people like and what they don't like. You can borrow some of their methodology in conducting your own in-depth research.

For example, if a prospect is using a competitive product, you could ask: "What is it you like about that product?" Listen for the answer. Then ask, "What is it you don't like about it?" Again listen. Now you have some important information. Perhaps you can provide greater satisfactions in whatever it is they like. Or you may be able to help them avoid something they don't like. Besides, you are not putting yourself in a position of knocking the competition. They told you in what way the competitor is lacking.

Questions to Avoid

Whatever you do, please don't ask questions in an opener that have such blatantly obvious answers that they sound more like scolding and are sure to offend, such as:

You do want to lower your costs, don't you?

You do want to safeguard your family's health, don't you?

With questions like these two in an opener, you are likely to have prospects doing things you are not going to appreciate. And their reasons will be emotional, having nothing to do with the logical merits of what you sell. You can't offend and persuade at the same time. Those questions may be all right in a summary statement when you are closing a sale, but please, not in an opener.

A Powerful Mind Opener

There is an inoffensive way to phrase questions that will prompt people to admit they could be receiving an important benefit or at least that you have something worth looking at. It is an effective way of keeping a prospect's mind open when it is heading toward a closed direction. It is known as the contingency question, sometimes called the just-supposing question. With this method you suggest a hypothetical situation and ask if a benefit would result from it or if it would be worth considering. For example:

Just supposing you had a machine that could perform this operation. Would it appreciably lower your costs?

Just supposing there is an important new discovery that thousands have acclaimed to be an important safeguard to their family's health. Would you be willing to take 15 minutes to learn about it?

Just supposing you took the time to list all the benefits your customers enjoy as a result of buying from you. And just supposing you did some creative brainstorming and composed "just supposing" questions to go with each one. Wouldn't that give you more opportunities to present your offering on a more favorable basis?

Other Ways to Keep Yourself out of Trouble

In addition to asking questions, another indirect approach to helping people discover their needs is to bring in a third party. This could be a quote from a person likely to be respected by your prospect or an article from a newspaper or magazine. It could be a story about another person, perhaps one of your customers who struggled with a problem until you came along and solved it. Let your prospects identify with the third party. Thus it is not you who suggests that they have the same problem.

When newspapers and magazines want to draw attention to a problem they wait until somebody does something about it, then tell the story. Throughout history the most effective communicators were storytellers. The Bible is full of stories and parables that bring concepts to life. Most people would rather hear stories about other people than about things or abstract concepts.

When you finish your third-party's story or statement, ask an open-end question such as:

How do you feel about this?
What has been your experience in this regard?

Quoting other people is an especially effective way of making what you say believable. It doesn't put you in a position of taking a stand that needs to be defended. Rather, you are in the position of a reporter relating what someone else said. Your prospects are less likely to disagree since you are attributing the remark to a neutral third party who is not there to sell something. However, if they happen to disagree, you can respond noncommittally with such remarks as, "Oh," or "Really," or "Hmm," and thus avoid getting into an argument. Instead, you can take another tack.

Keep Your Antennas Out

Keep your eyes and ears alert for quotes and stories. Read trade publications in your industry and your customer's industry with an eye for quotes and articles that are relevant. The more you do it, the more interested you become and your antennas become more finely tuned. Speaking of telling stories and asking questions, do you remember Anna Mae Randall, Harry, Ed Posnan, Jim Tucker, Bob Komasinski, Hotshot Charlie, Fred Hawkins, Jerry Clement, Professor Harold Hill, and Pion the warrior? Did they help you get a better handle on some abstract concepts? How do you feel about that?

Remember to be tactful in helping others become aware of their needs. You use tact when you quote a third party, tell a story, or ask questions in such a way that prospects state their needs in their own words.

How to Perfect Your Skill

Asking questions is a skill. Like any other skill it will improve with practice. But don't confine your practice only to selling situations. Get in the habit of asking questions in all of your interpersonal contacts with friends, family, and fellow employees. Plan to spend some time with others, in a social evening or luncheon, when you make a special effort to avoid talking about yourself. Instead, ask questions that will communicate sincere interest in the people you are with. Keep in mind the suggestions in this chapter. Your companions will find you to be a much more interesting conversation partner. You will feel better about it and about your improved communication skill.

9

Listening—The Other Side of a Question

A Lesson Learned Too Late

Glen Mobrey was in a state of utter shock. After 20 years of what he thought was a successful marriage, his wife asked him for a divorce.

"Well, we had the usual little disagreements," he related. "Doesn't everybody? But I hadn't the slightest inkling Dee was so unhappy that she wanted to call it quits. You know, I worked extra hard to earn the kind of money to give her everything I thought she ever wanted. But I didn't realize until it was too late that I didn't give her the one thing she really wanted above all the rest. I just didn't listen to her."

A Lesson Learned in Time

One of the greatest lessons I ever learned was taught to me by my daughter, Jill, when she was sixteen. I was known as a tough disciplinarian in those days. "Saturday night curfew is midnight," I would pronounce. "Not 12:15 or even 12:05, because if it were 12:05 I would have said 12:05 instead of midnight."

One warm summer evening it wasn't until a few minutes to 1:00 A.M. when a car finally pulled into the driveway. Her date must have seen me standing on the porch, under the light, with my arms sternly folded. He wasted no time shifting into reverse and screeching out of the driveway.

Jill gave me a cheery "Hi, Dad," as she lilted into the house. I was ready to go into the riot act routine but for some strange reason I kept my mouth shut. We sat down in the living room and she began to tell me all about her evening—what other kids did, what they said, how they felt, what was important to them. I hardly said a word except to respond to what was being said and ask some questions to clarify what I couldn't understand. It was a most absorbing conversational experience for me.

"Holy cow!" I finally said, "it's after three, and we've got to get up for church tomorrow. By the way, you know you were late."

"Yes, I guess so."

"What do you suppose we should do about that?"

"I suppose I should get grounded for a while."

Well, I don't think she ever was grounded as a result of that night. But the next morning she said to her mother, "Gee, Dad and I really had an interesting talk last night."

Interesting for me? Oh, yes! I got to know my daughter and to understand her generation in new and important ways. But over and above that, I learned how vital it is to a relationship to take the time to shut up and listen.

In Chapter 8 the importance of asking questions was emphasized. Listening is the other side of questions. Unless the asker listens, the questions have no meaning.

Reactions to Poor Listening

Have you ever had someone ask you questions and it became obvious to you they were not listening to the answer? To make matters worse their eyes were flitting around to other sights and sounds they didn't want to miss. How did you feel about that?

Sorry I can't be there to listen to your answer to my question but it's fairly safe to assume you don't feel very good about people who treat you that way. It is also safe to assume that your prospects are not going to feel very good about salespeople who don't actively and diligently demonstrate their willingness to listen.

In the Bible there's a story about Samson killing 10,000 Philistines with the jawbone of an ass. Every day thousands of sales are killed with the same weapon—by salespeople who won't shut up and listen.

An Important Aspect of Communication

Whenever I deal with the subject of communication in my seminars, I ask my audience what they would like to learn from that session. These are typical answers:

How to make a presentation.
How to write effective letters.
How to speak to a group.
How to use humor.
How to talk on the telephone.
How to convince people who disagree.
How to handle complaints.
How to reprimand unsatisfactory performance.

Almost never does anyone expect to learn something about listening. Yet, that is going to be the subject of a major portion of my seminar presentation. Communication is a two-way street. In oral communication, listening is 50 percent of the action.

Attitudes More Important Than Skills

There are skills that can be taught to help people listen more effectively. But before skills learning can take place, communication trainees must first become aware of the need to improve listening skills. Secondly, they must cultivate a sincere willingness to listen.

Several organizational training directors have told me about their experience conducting comprehensive listening skills training programs. They would spend days practicing the skills. It was drill, drill, listen, listen. By the time the course was finished they were up to their eyeballs in listening. The last thing they wanted was to do more listening. Yet without *wanting* to listen, these skills are practically useless.

Surpass Natural Inclination

Listening appears to be a passive process. After all everybody has two ears. Just do what comes naturally. What's the big deal?

The deal is that we talk at a rate of approximately 150 words per minute, but we can think close to 600 words per minute. That means that when someone talks to you, if you do what comes naturally, you will be thinking more words than what you hear. It is easy to become distracted. It is easy to pursue a line of thinking other than what your conversation partner is leading up to. To follow a natural inclination is to be thinking of what you are going to say next. If you are not careful you are apt to miss some of what is being said. In a sales situation, what you miss could be indispensable information. To make matters worse, the prospect is likely to sense that you're not really listening. Because doing what comes naturally is to nonverbally reveal what is going on inside of you. If you are impatient, bored, eager to express disagreement, or allowing your mind to wander, your prospect will know it. Result—the relationship is in jeopardy.

How to Listen Actively

So to avoid missing relevant information, to avoid jeopardizing relationships, be an active listener. Go beyond "doing what comes naturally" and make a deliberate effort to listen. Honestly try to gain an understanding of what is being said and of the feelings behind it. Show by your gestures and facial expressions that you are genuinely interested. Look at the person talking to you. Resist any temptation to shift your gaze to anything else that may be going on nearby. Take advantage of the extra thinking time afforded by the 450-word difference between speaking and thinking, and use this time to concentrate on what is being said. Use it to review and collect the bits and pieces together into a central idea. Use it to determine what is being omitted—to understand the feelings underlying what is being said.

If you do all of this, you certainly will avoid the fatal error of interrupting a person in the middle of a thought. The only people who don't mind being interrupted in the middle of a sentence are prisoners.

Dealing with the Long-Winded

At this point you may be thinking, "Hey Lee, I buy what you say about listening. It sounds good in theory, but what about prospects who ramble on with irrelevant detail or who switch from one point to another? It's hard to make any sense out of what they are saying. Then the time they are willing to spend with you runs out before you get an opportunity to state your case."

Yes, that does happen, perhaps more often than we would like. We can lessen our distress in these situations knowing that we have established rapport with a prospect by being a good listener and that we left the door open for a return visit.

This line of reasoning makes more sense with telephone contacts than it does with personal calls. Personal calls are expensive and getting to be more so in our inflation economy. If the call is away from the home base or off the beaten track, it could be a long time before that prospect is going to be available to see you on a return visit. Then there is a matter of timing. By the time you get back there the competition may have become entrenched, the prospect's needs may have changed, or any of a number of things could have happened to lessen your advantage.

Make the Most of Your Presence

Your biggest advantage when you're in the presence of a prospect is that you are already there. You have surmounted the tasks of getting through any screen of receptionists, secretaries, or assistants. The prospect is not out of town, in a meeting, or otherwise preoccupied. You don't have to arrange an appointment or work at getting attention. All of this is an accomplished fact. Do what you can to make the most of having completed all of those steps.

In other words, don't be too quick to settle for merely establishing rapport and leaving the door open for a return visit. This visit may be your best opportunity.

How to Shorten the Long Wind

Even though you are faced with a person who rambles on, be a good listener. Make a conscious effort to avoid showing impatience, boredom, or indifference. Wait for a completed thought or a break in the monolog. Then unobtrusively direct the conversation back in line with your objective. If you fail in the first attempt, listen intently for the next chance.

Another way to exercise initiative in setting the direction of a conversation is to ask a closed-end question pertaining to something the prospect said. Be ready to pick up the conversation as soon as the answer is given. Tie your remark to the answer. Then use it as a transition back to the point you want to discuss.

For example, let's suppose you are selling an advertising program that is built around a promotion to build store traffic for merchants in a shopping center. Halfway through your opening remarks to a prospect, let's call him Mr. DeBate, he interrupts you to go off on a tangent about the lack of business caused by "those stupid politicians running the government and their idiotic economic programs." While DeBate has the floor, your advertising program is out the window and politics is in.

Mr. DeBate ends a sentence with, "And I'll never vote for him again." Here's the cue for you to jump in quickly with your closed-end question.

"I take it you voted for him in the last election?"

"Yes, unfortunately."

"Well," you pick up, "I guess we're stuck with him till the next election but I don't think it's a good idea to let the things we can't do prevent us from doing the things we can do. Now, we can't get rid of this administration for a while, but we can do something constructive to stimulate business in our own backyard and that's the reason I'm here, Mr. DeBate. . . ." Then get back to the purpose of your call.

How to Be Well Liked

You gave Mr. DeBate a chance to release some pent-up feelings. You gave him the courtesy of listening to his point of view without letting it get too far out of hand. You discreetly changed to another subject that should be of interest to him. Now he is more likely to return the courtesy and hear you out.

Listening may appear to be a passive function, but good listening is not. It takes awareness. It takes skill, and as with any skill it takes practice. At the end of the last chapter, it was suggested that you practice asking questions in social situations. Now include the ideas from this chapter in your social practice experiences. Especially notice how positively people will respond to your willingness to let them be heard. There are millions of people with a deep craving to have somebody share their thoughts and feelings, to be understood, to know that someone appreciates them enough to listen to them for a few minutes. Give them what they want. They will want to have you around. They will give you their friendship—and very often their business.

10

Planning
Your Opening Move

Defining Some Terms

The readers of this book are probably involved in a variety of selling situations. While some few may make quick, one-call sales based on a brief presentation or demonstration, it is safe to assume that most will require enough dialog to warrant arranging an appointment for a convenient time for prospects to give the dialog the necessary attention. The dialog usually involves probing for needs, an interview and a presentation of some length, responding to resistance, and gaining commitment.

This book is not intended to cover in great detail such things as closing sales and resistance after an attempted close. I am concerned only with setting up presentations on the right basis and dealing with opening resistance.

Some more complex selling situations involve several phases of contact over a long period of time. It would be impossible to detail every type of the various possibilities. The main purpose in setting forth the following sequence is to define some terms we will be using. Therefore, the sequence is given according to the most typical progression.

Here, then, is the sequence of events on a new contact up to the point of presentation:

1. *The opening statement.* This is sometimes called the opener. It consists of three parts:
   (a) Introduction of yourself and your company.
   (b) An opening benefit.
   (c) A request for an appointment.
2. *The prospect responds.* The response is usually one or a combination of several of these:
   (a) Interest. The prospect admits to a need and agrees to an appointment.
   (b) Indifference. Prospects are indifferent when they don't see a need for what you sell. They are often complacent or satisfied with their present situation.
   (c) Skepticism. Skeptical prospects are likely to have a need and know it but do not believe everything said regarding your claimed ability to satisfy their need.
   (d) Objections. Prospects responding with objections during the opener also are likely to have a need and know it. But they also know, or prejudge, something about you, your company, or your product and make some negative remark.
   (e) An indefinite appointment is made. That is, the prospect declines to set a specific time for an appointment and asks you to phone at another time to confirm it.
   (f) The prospect chooses to terminate the contact.
3. *Probing for needs.* When the prospect resists your opening request for an appointment, you then ask questions to discover needs, important factual information, as well as the emotional background that will help you decide how to proceed. Probing for needs is the primary technique for dealing with indifference, skepticism, and objections. More about that later. Even when the response to the opener is affirmative, you may probe to qualify the prospect according to your criteria.
4. *Offering benefit to satisfy the need.* When at least one important need is identified, suggest a benefit that corresponds with the need and again request an appointment.
5. *The presentation.* The presentation centers on proving you can satisfy the need, building desire and conviction, and closing the

sale, or in the case of a more complex selling situation, setting up a subsequent phase. Some salespeople prefer to call their presentation an interview when it is more of a give and take verbal exchange rather than mostly monolog. Some make a distinction between an interview and a presentation. The interview part is further dialog to get a better understanding of the prospect's situation, whereas the presentation is directed toward relating benefits, explaining features, offering proof or a demonstration, or showing a line of merchandise. Actually, probing for needs is in itself an interview, and the line between probing and the interview can get blurred. Sometimes, at your suggestion, or at the prospect's invitation, your presentation will be given immediately following the opener or probe. For all practical purposes that is an appointment. It just happened to be made on the spot.

One other thing may happen at any point in the preceding sequence. You may decide that the prospect is not a good one, or for some other reason choose to terminate the contact.

Needs or Wants

I often hear arguments about the difference between needs and wants. Some claim it's more important to sell to people's wants rather than needs. That may be true in selling something like a luxury automobile as opposed to the need for transportation. But for most practical purposes and certainly if you are selling to business firms or nonprofit institutions, the word *need* is more applicable.

Earlier in this book, in addition to *want*, I use the words *problem* and *dissatisfaction*. Depending on the situation, *want*, *problem, dissatisfaction,* and *need* all have useful connotations. For the sake of simplicity, I will use the word *need* to represent any of those four meanings except where the special connotation of another word will fit better.

To Phone or Not to Phone?

Often in my seminars, someone in the audience asks, "Is it better to phone for an appointment or walk in cold?"

That is a closed-end question. Better to ask these open-end questions: Under what conditions is it better to phone for an appointment? Under what conditions is it better to just walk in? How skilled are you using the phone? To arrive at the best answer for you, compare the advantages of using a phone with the advantages of in-person calls.

Advantages of Opening on the Phone

- The greatest advantage of telephoning is the convenience and speed with which you can reach the largest numbers of potential prospects. If you can quickly separate prospects from suspects or can quickly evaluate the relative priority you will want to assign to prospects, the phone is your primary tool.
- You don't need to be dressed for business.
- You save the cost of gas and car maintenance or travel tickets.
- You don't waste valuable selling time fighting traffic, traveling long stretches, waiting for public carriers, or sitting in reception lobbies.
- You can call anywhere in the world from anywhere else in the world at any time of the day.
- When buying patterns are seasonal or affected by sudden swings of market conditions, it may be impossible to cover your territory otherwise. Once, as I was conducting an all-day seminar at a flour milling company sales meeting, we had to interrupt it at 11:00 A.M. Everyone scattered to find telephones as a shock wave hit flour prices.
- You are not at the mercy of weather. And if you live in snow and ice country, you know what that means.
- You can take notes and use a script without the prospect knowing or being distracted by your action.
- When calling from your office, you have at your fingertips files and information that can be used quickly if necessary.
- It is easier to get to the point on the phone without seeming abrupt.
- The prospect focuses attention on the matter at hand rather

than on you. This is particulary helpful if you have any nervous mannerisms that can be distracting.

■ Not always but often, people will drop what they are doing to answer the phone. They may not allow an interruption on that same task for an unknown, in-person visitor.

Advantages of In-Person Openers

■ It is easier to terminate a phone conversation than it is to dismiss an in-person visitor. That is one reason why people are more ready to allow a phone call to interrupt their preoccupation.

■ You can see the prospect's body language, which often bears important clues to what is actually happening.

■ You have an opportunity to make observations of the prospect's physical property, the size of the operation, the names on doors. You can get information from employees, neighbors, and literature. Needs may be apparent that you could discern only by being there. Remember Fred Hawkins and the truckload of unfinished components in Chapter 5.

■ You may have a personal appeal that comes across only in a face-to-face contact.

■ There is an increasing trend toward telephone sell-ing—even computer-actuated, recorded voices. Buyers, executives, and their staff assistants, as well as the public at large, are becoming more sensitive to and sophisticated in resisting telephone approaches.

■ You may have striking visual material that would help to neutralize initial resistance.

■ There will be many opportunities in person when you will get "slide in" or "spot" presentations. That is, you will go right from the opener to the interview to the presentation and at times make a sale all in one call. Some of those prospects on the phone would have easily brushed you off. Others would have postponed setting the appointment, causing frustrating callbacks. Still others would have cooled off completely or bought from a competitor in the meantime.

- Making drop-in calls is sound time and territory management. When you are in a certain vicinity and have time between appointments, such calls can make excellent fill-in use of time.
- Many salespeople are temperamentally unsuited to sit for any length of time at the phone. It takes a special kind of discipline to keep an enthusiastic momentum going. Inexperienced phone salespeople and those who don't like to do it will spend an inordinate amount of time shuffling prospect cards or on other diversions. Discouragement can come quicker because turndowns come quicker. One must be prepared to deal with the special kind of stress that comes with extended telephone use.
- Unskilled phone salespeople often use ill-advised "cherry picking" methods when their situation does not warrant doing that. Cherry picking is classifying prospects into categories of cherries or pits. The cherries are those who offer little or no initial resistance. The pits are the difficult ones and are quickly dropped from the list. You may get by doing that if your field of prospective clients is unlimited and if each client is a one-time sale. But it doesn't make good sense if your market is specialized or if you have identified certain target prospects that offer great potential, especially if that potential involves repeat sales over many future years.

As you can see, whether or not to use the phone has no general right or wrong answer. For now, let's concentrate on in-person calls. Many of these principles will apply either on the phone or in person.

The Coming Attraction

The aim of an opener, then, is to arrange for the interview and presentation to take place under the most advantageous circumstances. It is important to keep this primary objective clearly in mind and not to get ahead of it prematurely.

Did you ever see a receiver in football start advancing downfield before having full control of the ball? What usually happens? You're right, incomplete pass or a fumble. Likewise in golf. Did you ever get caught looking ahead and muff a shot as a result? "Keep your eye on the ball" is a well-worn cliché. By some quirk of human nature, most of us have to make a disciplined effort to do that—to concentrate on one single step at a time.

The same holds true in the opening phase of a sale. Getting an appointment on the right basis is a sale in itself. It is critically important and requires intense concentration.

Openers may be compared to previews that advertise a movie. Their aim is to tantalize—to stir up enough interest and curiosity to make you want to come back and see the whole thing. If too much of the plot is disclosed, you might prejudge it in a way that would cool off motivation to come back. If it doesn't tell enough of what the movie is all about, that too will fail to arouse your desire to come back.

The same with a good opener. You need to guard against adverse prejudgment on the part of your prospects. Tell no more about your proposition than is necessary to arouse their interest and curiosity so that they will agree to arrange for the time necessary to learn all about it. It is usually a mistake to try to sell the product or tell them all about it in the opener phase. Of course, there will be opportunities for "slide in" interviews and spot presentations. On a cold call, however, you would ordinarily ask the prospect if it is convenient for him or her that you continue. So for practical purposes an appointment is being set. It just happened that it is set to immediately follow your opener. But until you do that, it is still the opening phase and your objective is only to set the appointment on the most favorable basis.

Make It Your Best

The most important word in the title of this chapter is *planning*. The best opener you can give is a planned opener. An unspoken question in a prospect's mind at this stage is, "Do I want to talk to this salesperson or not?" You need the best answer you can give. It's not likely that the best answer you can give will come spontaneously. There isn't a lot of time for prospects to grow to like you. It's the first impression that counts and it must be good. You don't have a second chance to make a first impression.

I observe a negative emotional reaction on the part of many salespeople to the word *canned*. And I certainly am not advocating word-for-word presentations unless they have proved to work best for you. But openers are something else. The words and the whole manner of approach should be carefully planned. You have only a few seconds to a couple of minutes to get a positive response. Why risk giving it anything but the very best performance you can create, learn, and test-prove? The words will be used over again many times. Much of your precious selling time is on the line. Any one contact may eventually be one of the biggest sales you ever make. Go with the best!

There are two types of temperament involved here. When something as important as an opener needs to be said, some people prefer to carefully select their words. Furthermore, they are disciplined enough to pay the price it takes to diligently rehearse them. Others, and probably a great majority of salespeople fall into this category, are unwilling to do so. This is especially true of those with extrovert tendencies. Carefully preparing and rehearsing what to say is contrary to their nature. It is difficult, boring, time-consuming, and ego-deflating. On the other hand, there is some self-satisfaction in believing one can ad-lib brilliantly and succinctly. True, some can. But they are indeed rare birds.

Payoffs Are Worth the Price

Which type are you? Compare the price you pay (of a little time and effort, planning, and rehearsing), against these advantages:

1. You will be more effective, setting more appointments, with right buying authority, under the most favorable circumstances.

2. It will be easier for you to give openers.

3. Your attention can be concentrated on observing the prospect's reactions. Less need to be thinking about what you're going to say. You will be able to listen better and observe nonverbal

signals. These give clues as to subsequent responses you make and directions to take.

4. A favorable impression up front will have long-standing favorable effects on the ensuing stages of making the sale.

5. You will be more confident and poised knowing that what you're doing and saying is your best shot. This will help to dissolve any traces of fear or call reluctance.

Avoid These Disadvantages

On the other hand, here are some disadvantages to ad-libbing openers:

1. They are usually longer and more rambling than necessary. Extroverted salespeople tend to be overfriendly and more talkative than good judgment would recommend in an opening situation. They are bent on selling themselves. Their reasoning is, if it could be done in one hundred words, then one thousand words should be ten times better. They don't realize that a busy, possibly less extroverted prospect may not be in the mood for that much friendliness and conversation. Nor do they realize how much quicker they would sell themselves if they got to the point with a benefit the prospect could quickly understand. And they don't realize how unlikely it is for prospects to have the patience to track the meaning of a long-winded monolog, how much more likely it is for them to prejudge negatively and dismiss the visitor in order to get back to their preoccupation.

2. Weasel words and phrases tend to creep in. Theodore Roosevelt is credited with coining the term to describe "words that destroy the force of a statement by equivocal qualification as a weasel ruins an egg by sucking out its content while leaving it superficially intact." *Might, maybe, perhaps* fall into this category. Phrases such as "I just happened by," "I was wondering if," "I think you ought to," and "Sorry to bother you, but. . . ."

3. *I*-oriented phrases, instead of *you*-oriented phrases, tend to predominate; for example, "I'd like to show you," "I want you to see."

4. Prospects will later recall a negative reaction to an opener. You destroy what you need most in a presentation—confidence on

their part that you know what you are talking about. They may have agreed to continued dialog out of curiosity or whim, but the effect of an otherwise, good presentation could be diminished.

5. When you must think about what to say, you are less able to keep all senses tuned in to the moment. Vital clues can be missed.

6. You are apt to experience a higher level of anxiety caused by using needless mental energy. Remember the fable of the centipede:

> A centipede was happy quite
> Until a frog in fun
> Said, "Pray, which leg comes after which?"
> This raised her mind to such a pitch,
> She lay distracted in the ditch
> Considering how to run.

Be a Pro

Selling is a profession. Other professions require vigorous, disciplined practice in vital skills. Could you imagine a surgeon ad-libbing through an operation—performing it differently every time to suit mood or whim? I wouldn't suggest that you climb on an operating table and put yourself in the hands of such a doctor. A skilled surgeon doesn't have to think about every movement. Likewise a professional athlete, airline pilot, musician—or a centipede.

Bill Gove, the dean of sales motivational speakers and founding president of the National Speakers Association, uses the phrase *effortless effort* to describe the physical, mental, and emotional state he wants to achieve in order to perform at his best in front of an audience. I was with Bill one day when he spent all morning rehearsing a speech he had given hundreds of times before and was to give again that day at a luncheon.

When I mentioned to Bill my surprise that he still works this hard, he replied,

> Even though I have over 35 years on the speaking circuit, I need
> to practice in order to perform at my best. But this is not unusual.
> I've always been interested in what makes for "star quality

performance" in any field, be it sports, entertainment, business, whatever. It will always include desire, tremendous energy, and persistent hard work. I practice so my audience will be more comfortable with me. But moreover, so that I will be more comfortable with me.

Be Comfortable with Yourself!

What a great inspiration for salespeople to learn their craft. Especially when it comes to the all-important business of performing an effective opener. Yes, it is important that we work at helping prospects to be comfortable with us during that crucial moment. But it is more important that we are comfortable with ourselves. We either pay the price of working at developing a strong, smooth opener, or pay the price of losing opportunities to sell in order to indulge in spontaneous mutterings that often fail to get the job done. That is a far greater price. It takes a lot less time to learn to do it right than the time lost making calls that are unproductive.

Make It Sound Spontaneous

The most legitimate reason for not memorizing anything to be said is that it sounds like an elementary school student reciting something in class. True, it often does. But it doesn't have to. Herein lies the essence of professionalism. A pro not only works at learning the words, but also works at making it sound conversational and spontaneous.

An Important Tip for Conversational Sound

A common and glaring error that inexperienced speakers make with memorized material is in the way the articles *a* and *the* are pronounced. In conversation, most people pronounce *a* with a short sound as the *u* is pronounced in *up*. *The* is pronounced with the same sound unless the very next syllable is a vowel. Then it is pronounced *thee*.

But when a piece is being read, the *a* often gets a long sound as in *way*. Most readers will pronounce *the* as *thee* regardless of whether or not a vowel is the immediately following sound. In conversation, the *thee* sound only comes out when a vowel follows. Otherwise, it gets a short sound. Since memorized material is usually learned from reading a written script, the tendency is to pronounce *a* and *the* with long sounds even though the same person would pronounce it differently in conversation.

Singing an Opener Is for the Birds

Another common difference between written, subsequently memorized material and normal conversation is that the memorized material tends to take on a sing-song quality. This probably stems from recitation habits acquired in earlier school years. Listen closely to airline cabin attendants as they read the preflight safety instructions. You will hear a melody actually being sung. Talk to them later—no more melody. It doesn't happen in normal conversation.

How to Choose Words

Write the words you plan to use on paper. Composing words to sound conversational begins with the way a script is written. Write words to the script as spoken words rather than written words. There is a difference. Written words tend to be more formal. Bigger words are used that would not ordinarily be used in conversation.

We learned to speak before we learned to write. Speaking is a natural means of communication. Writing is synthetic. Therefore, spoken words sound natural, written words sound contrived unless special effort is given to making them sound natural.

As you compose the scripted words, close your eyes. Compose the words in your mind as you imagine speaking them. Then open your eyes and put the words on paper. Spoken words are not necessarily as grammatically precise as written words. Grammatical precision or freedom is an individual thing. It must be something you are comfortable with. Some people speak with more precision than others.

Use words you would naturally use in spontaneous speech. Work at making it sound just as though it was coming right off the top of your head.

Audio cassette recorders are an inexpensive, convenient, and effective tool in helping you to polish your delivery. Record your opener. Listen to the playback. Are you using bigger words than you naturally would? Is there a sing-song quality that shouldn't be there? Just by identifying it, you are a long way toward eliminating it. Check the way you pronounce the articles *a* and *the*. Is that the way you always pronounce them?

Have a friend, your spouse, or your manager critique the recording until he or she agrees that it sounds like the natural, spontaneous you. Then listen to it over and over until it becomes a natural part of you., If you spend a lot of time behind the wheel of your car, this is an excellent time to put your recorder to work.

Much of my time is spent in airports and on airplanes. I always carry a pocket-size recorder with an earplug. It's an easy way for me to learn new speech and seminar material. It's not even necessary to listen with complete concentration. The words and the vocal inflections register on the subconscious through sheer repetition.

Video recording equipment is now quite common and inexpensive. If you have access to it, so much the better. As a training and coaching tool, I find it unbeatable. Its advantages are obvious.

Let us proceed on the basis that you agree with the importance of carefully selected words in your opener and go about selecting those words.

That's what the next chapter is all about.

11

Putting Words Together

Spotlight the Benefit

Recall the three parts of an opener: (1) introduction of yourself and your company, (2) an opening benefit, (3) a request for an appointment.

The first part, the introduction of yourself and your company, requires no unusual creative effort. You've been doing this for years. It's best to use words that come easily and naturally to you. A telephone introduction, however, does require a special approach that will be dealt with in a later chapter. But in person, no big deal. In fact, some sales managers train their reps to not even introduce themselves at first when making in-person calls, rather get right into the benefit. Their feeling is the rep's identity is of little importance compared with the benefit. Hence, don't say anything that will take the spotlight off the benefit.

Yes, the most important consideration is the opening benefit. It gives the prospect a reason for wanting to listen to you. It's a good idea to review Chapters 5, 6, and 7 to get a better understanding of why certain words and phrases would be most effective. Remember that people do things for their reasons not yours. They are not going to be interested in what you sell or the fact that you want to sell it. They will be interested only in what good it could do for them. And as you are saying your opening lines, their immediate interest is deciding whether or not *talking to you* any further would be of any benefit to them.

Avoid This Common, Weak Opener

In all my years of working with salespeople in the field training, coaching, evaluating performance, one of the most common opening lines I hear after the introduction is ordinarily one of the weakest! "Could I have a few minutes of your time?"

What kind of benefit is that? For busy people, reaction to the thought of giving a few minutes of their time to a total stranger without good reason is bound to be negative. Of course, you must check to find out when it is convenient for a prospect to visit at length. Just don't make that your opening line in a face-to-face call. It belongs in the request for an interview but not your very first utterance.

Direct and Indirect Interruptions

An exception would be if, for some reason, you find it necessary to interrupt someone you can see is busy doing something else. This is known as a direct interruption. Even then, "May we talk for a few minutes?" is much better than "Could I have a few minutes of your time?"

An indirect interruption happens when you go through a third party such as a receptionist or a secretary. As the message is related to the person you want to see, chances are that person is busy doing something else at that moment. You will then have to wait in the outer lobby until it is convenient for your prospect to see you. So when you get face to face, you are expected to say something. You don't need to ask permission for initial time. You will need to ask for time only when you continue beyond the opener.

Going Beyond the Opener

Openers should be very brief. When you go beyond the opener, you are into an interview or a presentation. Before you get that far, make sure you're doing it with some indication of the prospect's compliance. To make sure of that, it's best to ask for time outright. But the time to ask for it is after you state a benefit, not in the opening line, unless it is a direct interruption. Other poor opening lines are:

> I just happened to be in the neighborhood . . .
> I was wondering if you might be interested in . . .
> I wanted to visit with you for a few minutes about . . .
> I'd like to get your business . . .

Again, what benefits are expressed or implied in those statements? Obviously none. To make a call just because you're in the neighborhood is to apologize for it. Busy people don't care much what strangers are wondering or what they want. Besides, all those opening lines are *I*-oriented.

Important Words to Use

One of the most important words to use is the name of the person you are talking to. There is no sweeter music to the ears of most people than the sound of their own name. Be sure you pronounce it correctly. Don't be shy about asking for the correct pronunciation. You're not going to offend anyone. Rather, the person will be pleased that you are taking the trouble of getting it right.

Find Answers to This Question

Then, going from the prospect's name as a start, ask yourself this question: Why should this person listen to me? Sit down and write as many answers to that question as you can think of. Do some creative brainstorming. When possible do this with other salespeople in your company. Two or more minds make a strong creative force. Remember the rules of brainstorming—go after a large quantity of ideas. No criticism or negative comments allowed during the idea-generating time. Do your judging and refining later. You are bound to come up with plenty of good answers to that critical question, "Why should this person listen to me?" Compose your answers in such a way as to paint word pictures of benefits—the more specific to the prospect's world, the better. How you can help them to function more effectively, assure their survival, help them keep pace with the rapidly changing times; increase productivity; make more profit; cut costs; improve morale, internal communications; reduce accidents, down time, rejects; attract, satisfy, and keep customers; avoid mistakes, wasted effort, legal problems, losing key employees; make more effective use of time; get more enjoyment out of work and life; avoid criticism, ridicule, fear, illness, death, pain, worry, embarrassment; or profit from any special benefits your product offers.

Specific Benefits Best

The aforementioned are all general benefits. Better to translate them or attach them to something specific in the prospect's world. For example:

1. Cut costs by reducing hours of labor at least 50 percent on the assembly of the model 102 gear box.
2. Increase profits by creating a whole new market for model 102.

Stay away from threadbare clichés such as, "This is the best buy," "We are the greatest," "We are the fastest growing," "Acclaimed the world over." Such meaningless superlatives suggest that anything else you say is going to be meaningless and overstated.

An Especially Powerful Word

There is an extremely versatile and powerful four-letter word—a clean four-letter word—that works wonders in virtually any opener. Of the many different products all of my clients or I personally have been involved in selling, I have never known of a product for which it does not apply. It in fact replaces the word that stands for any product. It is that universal. Its very use automatically implies a benefit!

The word is *idea*.

No matter what you sell, there must be some ideas connected with how it is used, or purchased, or financed, or sold, or something. Somewhere from your experience with other customers, or from reports that you heard from others in your company, or from an article in a trade magazine, you must know of a unique or especially creative use of your product that can become a special idea—*an idea that provides a benefit*. It's an idea that will make the prospect more money, cut costs, or do a job easier, faster, or whatever.

At the moment you introduce yourself, a prospect may not even be remotely interested in buying your product. But he or she will be likely to be interested in considering an idea that will offer a solution to a problem, or provide some special benefit. Ideas are such powerful things. All the marvels of our space age, all of our modern conveniences, today's medical miracles, all creation for that matter, first were ideas. It has been said that small minds discuss people. Average minds discuss events. Great minds discuss ideas.

But don't be like the sales rep who opened with, "Mr. Prospect, I have an idea that can make you a whole lot of money."

The prospect motioned toward a chair saying, "Come in and sit down. I'm always willing to listen to ideas like that. What's your idea?"

"Well, I really don't have one, but wasn't that a heck of an opener?" the wag replied.

Be sure you have a solid idea, well planned, backed up with proof that relates to a prospect's self-interest.

A Two-Way Call Objective

A good way to introduce your idea is to make the introduction of it an important part of your call objective and declare it as such to your prospect. Your opening benefit would start out something like this: "My special reason for calling on you today is to show you an idea that. . . ." What you have then is a two-part call objective, one for you, one for the prospect. Yours is to arrange an opportunity to present and eventually sell your product. The prospect's is to learn about an idea that will be of benefit.

Furthermore this automatically makes the opener *you*-oriented. It gets your attitude pointed in the right direction toward the prospect's self-interest. It will be especially attention and interest grabbing when a salesperson who came to call just before you said, "I just happened to be in the neighborhood," or some other weasel-worded, apologetic, I-oriented remark.

Bring in the Witnesses

Immediately following the word *idea* and before you reveal the benefit, another potent and convincing phrase is, "Our customers tell us," or, "Our customers find." Instead of *customers* you may prefer the word *clients*, or there may be special terminology in your industry. For example, in the trucking business customers are called *shippers*. In the seed industry it is *growers*.

This magic phrase packs a considerable amount of believability into your benefit statement. A prospect would rightly expect you to make positive claims about your product. But now it isn't a claim you are making. You're like a reporter relating a claim made by a neutral third party who doesn't have any self-serving motive in helping you to reach your objective. Anyone would have to admit a measure of stubbornness to not open the mind at least a little bit after hearing such an endorsement.

Joining the Benefit Phrases

Now you have a simple formula to showcase an interest-catching, opening benefit:

1. The prospect's name.
2. A special reason for the call.
3. An idea.
4. "Our customers tell us. . . ."
5. Provides a specific benefit.

A complete opening benefit would go something like this:

> Mr. Washington, my special reason for calling on you today is to show you an idea that our customers tell us reduces hours of labor by at least 20 percent on the assembly of gear boxes similar to the one on your model 102.

In that statement the words *cut cost* aren't even necessary. They would be redundant. They are translated into a specific benefit. I can't imagine anyone on whom you would use this opener not immediately recognizing the general benefit.

It is not necessary to link a feature of your product to the benefit you are leading with in your opener. Talking about features, proving why benefits happen, belongs in the presentation, not in the opener. Putting features in your opener is going too far, too fast, making it more complicated, harder for the prospect to follow, risking prejudgment. Your best opener will hold a spotlight on the benefit—the end result. The only time to talk about a feature in the opener is when the feature is something extraordinary that would arouse curiosity or for some other reason would merit sharing the spotlight with the benefit.

Optional Phrasing

Details in your situation may vary from those presumed in the above example. That may require some alternative phrasing. For example, you may have a brand-new product that does not yet have a customer track record. Then instead of quoting a satisfied customer, get an opinion of a prominent authority in your field. Or say, "That has been tested and proved to . . . [solve a particular problem that is common to your clientele]."

Another likelihood is that you don't know the specific details of a prospect's possible needs. In that case you would give a less specific benefit with the expectation of doing some probing to uncover a specific need in the interview phase. Your opener would then go like this:

> Mr. Washington, my special reason for calling on you today is to
> show you an idea that our customers tell us reduces hours of labor
> in some manufacturing processes by as much as 20 percent.

In many instances you will have a pretty good idea what the prospect's needs are. Your product is designed and being sold to meet some kind of need, otherwise it wouldn't exist. You're calling on people facing similar problems. Making more profit is universal in business. Cutting costs has an even wider range of need.

Close for an Appointment

After you give the benefit statement, the next part of your opener is to request an interview and a presentation. This could be scheduled immediately following the opener if the prospect's time allows and if other considerations suggest it's the right basis. Or you would set an appointment for another time. It's a good idea to let the prospect know approximately how long it would take.

Putting It All Together

A complete opener with all three parts together would be:

Mr. Washington, my name is Pat Murphy with Acme Corporation. Mr. Washington, my special reason for calling on you today is to show you an idea that our customers tell us reduces hours of labor at least 20 percent on the assembly of gear boxes similar to the one on your model 102. You could evaluate this in about 20 minutes. Do you have the time now or would one o'clock this afternoon be better?

Suggest Time and Date

When closing for an appointment always be ready to take the initiative in suggesting a time and date. In the preceding example, instead of suggesting the specific time, supposing you had asked, "When would it be convenient for you to take a look at this idea, Mr. Washington?" It's a good bet you would get a reply something like, "Give me a call in a couple of months." At that time, your visit would be forgotten and you'd have to start from scratch.

Notice, too, in the last example, alternative choices of time were suggested. This gets the prospect thinking *when* rather than *if* the appointment will be granted. *When* is an easier decision to make for a person who has any lingering doubts.

Buyers Dislike Special Effects

There was a time when sales reps were taught to schedule appointments at odd times such as 9:02 or 10:26. Stay away from such cutesy tricks. Reasonable, experienced buyers know you are doing it for effect. They don't like anything done to them for effect.

Give them credit for knowing it's unlikely, when scheduling appointments, that 9 o'clock or 10:30 would make any difference.

When Your Benefit Misfires

Occasionally the benefit you lead with will be off target. For example, supposing Mr. Washington was planning to phase out his model 102, or it was being redesigned without a gear box. And you didn't know that. Then quickly switch to a general benefit. At least you are a lot closer to his interest than if you had "just happened to be in the neighborhood."

Qualifying Prospects

When you are not sure whether a suspect is a prospect or what that person's needs may be, take this approach:

> Mr. Lincoln, my company is serving many manufacturing firms with an idea that our customers find substantially reduces hours of labor on certain manufacturing processes. My special purpose in calling on you today is to find out if it would have an application to your business. Could I get your answers to a few questions?

When calling unannounced, especially on business executives, it is important to state a benefit before you begin to ask questions. Coming out of the blue from a stranger, a question is likely to be taken as meddlesome, and so resisted with a natural reaction of, "It's none of your business." Even when that is not spoken it could be a reaction in thought.

A benefit gives them justification for sharing information in addition to sharing time of the day with you. Taking this approach also helps you avoid sounding impertinent by making wrong assumptions about their needs.

Your first objective with this type of opener is to determine whether or not you have a prospect. Your second objective is to assign a priority to your prospect. Here are four criteria that generally mark prospects:

1. They have a need for your product.
2. They can afford to pay for your product.
3. Potential volume justifies your time and effort.
4. They would be receptive to your presentation.

You need to prepare questions that will give you a picture of how they stack up with those four points. A review of Chapter 8 will help you to do that.

How to Probe for Needs

Be especially mindful of using an indirect approach with your questions to encourage prospects to start talking about their needs. Bear in mind that it is not enough for you to find out prospects' needs. It is important that they discover what their needs are.

Suppose you were calling on a feed manufacturer to sell packaging. These would not be good questions with which to start the interview: "Do you need any bags today?" "Are you satisfied with your present source of supply?" "Do you have need for lower packaging costs?" It would be better to go about it indirectly:

You: How many fifty-pound bags do you ship in a month?"
Prospect: About 150,000.
You: How much are you paying per bag?
Prospect: Let's see, here's an invoice. Looks like seventeen cents per.
You: How do you feel about that price?
Prospect: Well it's been going up like everything else. I guess it's getting to be more than I'd like to pay.

Now you have uncovered a need—dissatisfaction with the price being paid to a present supplier. The need was uncovered indirectly, in a way that made it easier for the prospect to reveal and less likely to deny later.

Of course, you would take this tack assuming you had some ideas about lower-cost packaging. Once a need is isolated in the interview, you know what direction your presentation must take to make a sale. You will build it around benefits that relate to the need.

When They Are Buying from a Competitor

If you sell a product that gets repeat sales from buyers, you probably have prospects who are buying from competitors and are susceptible to change through a better idea. One thing you don't want to do is directly knock the competition. That implies that the buyer made a mistake and will tend to cause defensiveness.

An indirect approach allows prospects to arrive at a notion that it would be a good idea to evaluate their present source. And there you are ready to help them follow through on their own notion.

Begin your probing for needs with a closed-end question. Such questions are easier to answer and provide for a warmup to the more thought-provoking, feeling-finding, open-end questions.

How to Set Up a Needs Analysis

To determine needs for some products, it is helpful or even necessary to conduct an inspection of the prospect's operation or physical plant, to interview employees, or something of that nature. Bear in mind that many organizations spend big bucks for consultants to do what you are doing free of charge. Then your opener following the introduction part would go something like this:

> Mr. Lincoln, we are working with many companies similar to yours that were amazed to discover the amount of money they were losing each day because of needless or improper maintenance. My special reason for calling on you today is to get permission to survey your operation to see if we can suggest some ideas that will reduce your maintenance cost.

The Power of "Trouble in River City"

In the above example, reference to the salesperson's customers was put before "my special reason. . . ." This presents an opportunity to put emphasis on a typical, potential problem. This is the "trouble in River City" concept covered in Chapter 7. Heed its compelling power!

When their mental awareness is attuned to avoiding criticism, ridicule, disapproval, pain, financial loss, and fear, most people are most strongly motivated to take action than when it is attuned to gaining pride, pleasure, profit, or feelings of security. Sure, it sounds nicer the other way around. And I'm certainly not a cynic. It is true that some are motivated for loftier reasons, and to think that everybody is at all times would be a nobler, however unrealistic, thought. The idea that we can be motivated by fear may bother some readers of this book. But call after call, week in and week out, when it comes to human motivation, the odds are always in favor of avoidance behavior. Remember the example in Chapter 6 about your reaction to someone on your lawn at 3:00 A.M. with a fifty-dollar bill, compared with your reaction to someone stealing a fifty-dollar chaise lounge.

Or try this experiment. Ask a few people who smoke whether they would like to quit. When you hear yes, ask, "Why don't you?" Chances are you will hear, "I enjoy smoking."

But this usually is not true. With smokers who would like to quit but don't, the reason they don't is they can't stand the pain of withdrawal. For most smokers, what they think is pleasure is really avoidance behavior. The truth is, they continue smoking to avoid the withdrawal pain even though they want to quit.

Remember, the problem must be in the prospect's mind before a solution would begin to be considered. When you come to call, it would be a rare instance that someone would happen to have in mind the problem for which you have a solution. It's your job to put it there. That is what selling is about.

As you plan the words to use in your opener think of all the problems, needs, dissatisfactions your present customers have had for which your product provided solutions. Think of the possible similarities in each prospect's situation. Get ideas from your manager, other salespeople selling the same product. Do some creative brainstorming. Think of ways these problems can be highlighted in your opening statement. You will find the ideas you generate to be truly magic door openers.

When They Want More Information

Prospects often will respond to your opener by asking questions such as, "What is this all about?" or "Could you tell me more about what this is?" They haven't yet agreed to set an appointment. Nor do they give any indication the dialog will be allowed to continue for any length. In fact, they seem to expect a one-liner for your answer so they can quickly decide whether or not to hear more.

Be prepared for this. So far you are still in the opener phase—
the coming attractions. Avoid saying anything that may cause unfa-
vorable prejudgment. Don't begin a full presentation with anything
less than what you know is the right basis. It helps when your
presentation includes a demonstration or visual material. Then you
can say:

> Mr. Lincoln, I wish I could tell you all about it in just a word or
> two. But you will be able to evaluate it a lot faster by seeing it. It
> would take just 20 minutes for you to determine whether or not
> this would be profitable for your firm. Shall we do that now or
> would one o'clock this afternoon be better?

They may press you further, insisting on more detail. Try to phrase
your answers by placing emphasis on what your product will do for
them, rather than describing the product. Even though they seem
to press for the answer to "what is it?" You know in your heart that
they are really not interested in that. They are interested only in the
benefits it will provide.

Imagine an insurance agent selling a pension and profit-sharing
plan. The prospect asks, "But what is it?" If the answer were simply,
"life insurance," the door is likely to be closed very quickly with,
"Not interested." At any given moment, most people are not
interested in buying life insurance. But they would be interested in
saving tax dollars. If it happens that life insurance is used to fund a
tax-deductible retirement plan, that's fine. However, it is only
accepted as fine after the tax-deductible benefits are understood.
The agent is not doing the prospect a favor by answering the "what
is it" question directly. That person may go through life never
realizing how many needless tax dollars were being spent.

A good way to reply to "what is it?" is to begin with, "for
example," then go into a story about how one of your customers
benefited from your product. Better still, preface the customer's
benefit by telling how the customer struggled with a problem—how
miserable he felt, how much money he was losing, how much
"trouble in River City there was." Then you came along. The sky
cleared. The sun came out, and they lived happily ever after.

OK, you may think, that's a bit much. And for some situations,
you may be right. But the classic storytelling formula is:

1. Here they were. (conflict, struggle, pain, problem)
2. Here is what they did. (solution)
3. Here they are now. (problem solved)

Billions of dollars are spent every year on advertising using that formula. You've seen the scenario hundreds of times. It goes something like this:

"What's the matter, Ed? You look down in the dumps."

"Well, you know Charlie—pain, itch, swelling."

"Have you tried Formula X?"

"Does it really work?"

"It sure does. Doctors recommend it."

Next scene, another day:

"Gee, Charlie, you were right! The pain, itch, and swelling are gone. I feel like a new person thanks to you and to Formula X."

Take a tip from your advertising brethren. Go ye therefore and do likewise.

Please don't interpret up-front questions by prospects as being objections. Questions are a positive sign. It means you've struck interest. That's good. Curiosity is a powerful stimulant to interest. Curiosity may have killed many cats, but lack of it has killed many sales. Curiosity is a main reason prospects will listen to you at all. Do whatever you can to encourage it!

Keep It Plainspoken

Be sure to choose words in your opener that are natural for you to say and that you are comfortable with. In my examples words such as *evaluate, permission,* and *needless* were used. Instead of *evaluate,* you might use *judge, test,* or *figure out.* Instead of *permission,* just the expression *OK* could sound more natural. In place of *needless* try *useless* or *unwanted.*

Even more important, choose words that your prospects easily understand and identify with as an important part of their world. I've heard insurance agents speak of capital conservation, capital needs analysis, and liquidity analysis. Although those terms refer to important benefits, some prospects might wonder where they would keep it if they ever bought it! Everyday English would be more easily understood, such as, "Let me take a look and see if you're not paying too much to Uncle Sam," or "Let's try to figure out how to make sure the ownership of your property stays with your family."

How to Use Referrals

Another good opener is a referral. Be sure you have permission to use the referrer's name and check to make sure the prospect will recognize it. On a business or professional call, it is best that your prospect can identify with the referrer in a similar business or professional situation and that the referrer is equal or higher in status. It wouldn't be a good idea to use the name of a low-ranked manager from a small company with a prospect who is a top-level executive of a large corporation. A referral would go something like this:

> Mr. Jefferson, my special reason for calling on you this morning is at the suggestion of John Adams of the Adams Company. He's been a customer of ours for several years and is pleased with ideas we created especially for him that he said helped develop some profitable new business. He felt sure you would be interested in considering what we have to offer.

One note of caution regarding referrals. Unless you have an unlimited supply of them, don't get hooked on referrals. I've known salespeople who are reluctant to make a new contact without one. They also let a lot of good selling time slip by while they are setting up referrals. Of course a referral is a good way to introduce yourself to a stranger, but not the only good way. You will be wise to use referrals as only one of several approaches in your opening repertoire.

With or without a referral, know that most people you will call on are basically courteous. They will be willing to devote a few minutes of their time to a courteous and sincere stranger who appears to offer at least an idea that could have merit.

12

Getting Through to Buying Authority

Beware of the Egress

Before P.T. Barnum went on the road with "The Greatest Show on Earth," he had already made a fortune with his American Museum in New York City. The museum became such a great attraction, patrons would bring their lunches and stay all day. Every day thousands would be lined up waiting to get in and spend their money, but they couldn't because the place had limited capacity and the crowd was not turning over fast enough.

So Barnum had a fancy, inviting passageway built. Above it a huge sign announced THIS WAY TO THE EGRESS. A continuous procession of curious people would walk through this passageway expecting to see another wonder of the world. As they walked through a door at the end of the tunnel, they found themselves out in an alley unable to get back in without paying another admission. There were always plenty at the front door eager to take their place. At least they added another word to their vocabularies when they found out that *egress* meant *exit*.

Does this story have anything to do with selling? It sure does! When you know the person you are calling on has the authority to buy yet fobs you off on someone who lacks authority, look out! It could be the way to the "egress." If you go for it too quickly, you are apt to find yourself on the outside with no sale. Or worse, the lower authority will have you believing he or she is doing a selling job on the inside for you. A lot of high-priority time can be invested in callbacks that end up nowhere.

A Common Error Salespeople Make

Observing my clients' salespeople in action during field work-outs with them and in discussing this matter with sales executives, I find that a common error of salespeople is to fail to make a persistent effort in convincing the right buying authority to agree to a sales interview. And conversely they tend to be too quick and eager to spend time with persons in the prospect organization who can say no but do not have the authority to say yes.

I don't mean to say you should slight or risk offending subordinates. There will be times when you will have no choice but to open and even present to them. And when you do, give them your best effort. Give them every courtesy you would give to Number One. Sometimes they have important influence in the final decision. There are situations in which several people at various levels in the organizational heirarchy are involved in the decision. By all means cultivate them with care. In such cases you probably know that it is necessary to sell in depth and you do it with planned intent.

But too often salespeople will carelessly or unwittingly allow themselves to be confronted with the persons who can't make a positive decision. And so, they end up with no more than frustration to show for their efforts.

When to Set the Stage

The critical time in setting up sales presentations on the right basis with proper buying authority is at the very first approach.

Keep the Odds in Your Favor

I happen to be a great believer in odds. There is a neat, predictable, mathematical precision to them. The multibillion-dollar insurance industry thrives on them. So does Las Vegas.

Unless you are sure a lower-level employee has the authority to make a buying decision for what you are selling, be aware that opening to him or her is to proceed at great risk.

Even under most favorable circumstances, you can sell only a certain pecentage of your prospects. Anything that affects those circumstances less favorably will also diminish your odds of making a sale. To make your objective anyone below the decision-making level has a serious diminishing effect on your odds. A batter in baseball can swing at pitches outside the strike zone and get a hit occasionally. But with every such swing, the batting average goes down.

Every time you make a call it's like stepping into the batter's box. Every time you open to the right person, you are taking a level swing at a ball that is in the strike zone. When you open to someone who can't make the decision you are going for a pitch outside the strike zone. You may, on occasion, make a sale starting out this way, but your ratio of sales to calls will go down. The net result will be precious selling time wasted—lower total sales volume.

If you agree that time is money—that in the sales profession you translate time into revenue for your company and into personal income—then the gambling tables of Las Vegas or Atlantic City would give you better odds for your money than you get from the monetary value of the time spent with the wrong person in a selling situation.

Identify the Key Decision Maker

Effective opening strategy, then, begins with identifying the key decision maker.

Selling to individual consumers does not present any identification difficulty. With a small company it is usually the owner or partners, except for routine purchases that may be delegated to an employee. A major purchase by homeowners may require the presence of both wife and husband. Make sure appointments are made to include all decision makers in a complete presentation even though the opener may be made to only one.

Who Rules the Roost?

But who is the key decision maker in a small business or in a family?

Irene Reinke sells home improvements. During the warm-up part of her presentation, while she is arranging some of her visual material and samples, Irene asks a question unrelated to her business such as, "Where do you folks like to spend your vacation?" She does not look directly at the couple as she asks it, instead busies herself with her props. Her reasoning is that she doesn't want to influence one or the other by indicating with her eyes which should answer. She then makes a special attempt to draw out the preferences—and get nailed-down agreements from the first that answers.

How to Approach Large Organizations

In the world of larger business firms and nonprofit institutions, we find a more complex hierarchy of decision-making influentials, with varying degrees of authority and varying degrees of isolation from unsolicited contact by salespeople.

There are no universal rules that apply to every kind of selling situation. Therefore the uniqueness of any particular one must be taken into account in customizing your approach.

Who Is Your Right Person?

Right persons have many different titles depending on what you are selling. Your experience, combined with the experience of other salespeople in your business, has probably sorted out the levels of buying influence to some extent.

If purchasing agents routinely make buying decisions for your product, they are easy to identify. But often P.A.s merely place orders for decisions made elsewhere in that company. Often, too, they won't tell you that. They may lead you to believe you are calling on the right person when they are in fact serving as screens protecting the real decision makers from spending time with salespeople. It is wise to do some sleuthing to find this out first before you go over the head of a P.A. Because if a P.A. is, in fact, the real decision maker, you must proceed very cautiously in making other contacts in that organization. Otherwise you can quickly wear out your welcome there. Sometimes it's not easy to get the truth regarding who the key influences are. It is such things that make selling such an interesting challenge.

Authority and responsibilities, regardless of title, vary widely from one organization to another, making it expedient to do some preliminary information gathering. This is true whether or not your prospective organization has purchasing agents.

Valuable Personal Characteristics

Your best bet for gathering such information is to develop a nose for this sort of thing. Keep your antennas out, your eyes and ears open to relevant bits and pieces of information. Some salespeople are naturally curious and observant. This comes easily to them. Others need to work at it harder.

I hope that reading Chapters 8 and 9 on questioning and listening techniques has helped to broaden your skill in this area of perceptivity and I hope you practice using these skills. Get in the habit of asking questions of receptionists, other employees of your prospects' organizations, neighbors of the prospects, other salespeople who call on them, or anybody who can shed some light on how buying decisions are made in that organization.

Evaluate Information-Gathering Time

As valuable as this information may be, be careful not to spend an inordinate amount of time gathering it. Remember the time clock syndrome, the tendency to view a job as a block of time to be filled with activities. Some salespeople will try to justify doing something other than facing the moment of truth—which is to be in direct contact with prospects and risk rejection, risk failure.

Another factor related to the time clock syndrome is the willingness to spend time with people having lower-level buying authority because they are easier to get in to see and are less likely to cause rejection.

Evaluate Your Intent

An important point is this: When you do spend time with lower-level influentials, especially when you make an opener to them, be sure that it is necessary or to your advantage and that it is done with your intent.

On the other hand, be sure you are not doing it because it seems easier or is less risk to your ego or because your opening technique is faulty. And never do it without making a carefully planned effort to avoid an impasse.

Approach the Decision Maker First

Even in cases where you know in advance that several people are likely to be involved in a buying decision, make every effort to first approach the person with the highest decision-making authority. There are several possible advantages to doing this.

In the first place, this right person may agree to a complete interview. This is more likely to happen if you are skilled in using an effective opener. So now you are right where you should be in the most advantageous position.

Second, Number One may introduce you to the lower-level person or persons, giving them instructions to hear your story. In this case, you will get preferential treatment and a higher degree of attention and interest than you would by starting at the lower levels.

Third, Number One may tell you just how much authority lower-level persons have, may even tell you that they can buy if they see fit. Whether they can or not, you will know exactly where you stand and be in a better position to figure out how to proceed.

Fourth, Number One may promise to listen to your complete presentation if lower level likes it but can't buy. It will require a second presentation on your part. But you are a lot better off than starting low and not being able to present directly to the decision maker. For once you start at a lower level, it is very difficult to go over that person's head up to the higher level without risking offense to your first contact. The alternative is to have the lower-level people do the selling for you up the ladder. Unfortunately, it would be impossible to train them to do anywhere near the kind of selling job you were trained to do. Besides, subordinates don't like to recommend spending money, nor do they like to take the responsibility for approving or requesting something that they could be criticized for later.

Remember Captain Miles Standish. He performed many brave deeds as leader of Plymouth Colony. But when he fell in love with Priscilla Mullens, he sent John Alden to propose to her for him because he didn't have the nerve to do it himself. He lost her as a result of his lack of assertiveness. Likewise, you can lose sales by depending on a go-between.

How to Deal with Lower Authority

If you happen to find yourself in the predicament of opening to someone who is interested in your proposal but can't make a buying decision, your best bet is to *sell* the idea of getting to the top person by citing the benefits of doing that. Say something like this:

> It's not fair for me to expect you to do the selling for me. May I suggest you set an appointment with your boss for the three of us to get together. This way you will get credit for recommending a good idea and I'll get credit for doing my job of selling. It will save time for all three of us, because I'll be able to share my experience on how this product is used by firms similar to yours and I'll be able to answer any questions either of you may have.

Why Persistence with the Right Person Pays

While it is true that occasionally sales are lost because lower-level people are offended by a salesperson's persistent effort to reach a top decision maker, many more are lost because of futile effort with people who can't buy. Your odds are in favor of persistent effort to reach the top.

So when you are in contact with the right buying authority don't be too quick to accept a brushdown to a lower level. You have the attention of the person who is privy to information lower levels may not have. Here is an opportunity to find out how decisions are made, who the decision makers are, and what their criteria are. In other words, you can find out what ground rules you will face.

How to Deal with a Brushdown

Try this tack:

Number One: You don't want to see me, you want to see George Fleming. He handles that.

You: Fine. If Mr. Fleming likes it and believes it's right for your firm, can he make the decision to buy it?

How Number One answers this question is even more significant than what is said. If the answer is yes, without any hesitation—with a firm, positive ring of certainty to it—Mr. Fleming is probably the right person.

If there is hesitation, any hedging, any elusiveness, anything in the way the reply sounds that gives you reason to doubt that Fleming is the decision maker, he probably isn't. Then you will be wise to do some further probing. Specifically, ask if Fleming would report back to Number One with a briefing and if the decision would then be made jointly.

But if the answer to your first question is no, you know who is really going to make the decision. You can also be pretty sure that the selling job Fleming makes to the decision maker will be nowhere near as complete and effective as yours would be.

More Benefits of Persistence

Other valuable information can be gained from Number One, such as when purchases are likely to be made, what the organization has done in the past, whether there is any competition lurking in the wings, what the organization likes about past experience or competitive products, what it doesn't like, what else is in the hopper, what the obstacles to your getting an order may be. Be sure to include open-end questions to get at feelings and attitudes that affect buying decisions. This kind of priceless information is more likely to be divulged at a higher level than by a subordinate who may not be certain about what is or is not confidential and may fear being held responsible for leaking information that shouldn't be freely given.

Besides, the added dialog may present an opportunity to convince Number One to take a firsthand look after all or be included in the interview with Fleming. Remember, the convincing job requires talking about benefits. In this case the benefits relate to what is in it for Number One by taking a firsthand look. Your presentation may contain some valuable information that Number One would profit from learning firsthand. It would save time for everyone concerned. Perhaps it is important that Number One is in the unique position to evaluate your proposal in terms of the overall operation. Or Number One is the person who can make an immediate decision and so avoid any delay in realizing benefits to the organization. Think of any other benefits unique to your product or service that can be emphasized here.

Keep the Right Door Open

If Number One still insists that you must deal with Fleming first, even though Fleming can't make a buying decision, say this:

> Of course, I will discuss this with anyone in your organization you want me to. But if Mr. Fleming likes it and believes it's right for your firm, would the door be open for me to come back and present it to you firsthand?

If the answer to this is yes, it will take two separate presentations, but you are on fairly solid ground going to Fleming next. However, if the answer is no, realize that your odds have fallen considerably.

How a Master Gets the Right Person

Tony Pernelli sells employee motivation programs. He makes his first opener to the president of prospective companies. Often the president will tell him that the personnel manager is the one he should see. But Tony knows from experience that personnel managers almost never have a budget for his type of program. The final approval usually has to come from the president. I watched Tony in action as he called on S.A. Amundson, the president of a medium-size manufacturing company. Here's how Tony got Mr. A to hear him out.

Mr. A: The person you should be talking to is Bert Dierks, the personnel manager. Employee motivation is his area of concern.

Tony: Well, Mr. Amundson, certainly Mr. Dierks should sit in with us, as I'm sure we could profit from his thinking. But, Mr. Amundson, I deliberately came to see you for three very good reasons. The first is, you, more than anyone else in your organization, are vitally interested in evaluating the cost-cutting effect my program can have on your P&L statement. Second, you are the one person here who could honestly be called unprejudiced toward a particular department, since you alone can see the whole operation, or the big picture. And that puts you in the best possible position to know almost immediately whether or not what I have can help you cut costs. And third, Mr. Amundson [at this point Tony has a big smile on his face], you are the one person in the organization who can make an immediate decision, and we both know how expensive procrastination can be.

When using these techniques, be sure to take it easy and keep your good humor. Remember, you are a guest in the domain of one who is accustomed to calling the shots there. Don't let the firmness of your suggestions appear to be a demand. Make it clear that you are stating your terms, but the decision to grant the interview is entirely in the hands of the prospect. Establish the fact that you are a high-grade individual of equal business stature. Your manner must show that you have full confidence in what you are selling, that you know from previous experience your proposal is valid and will be of benefit to the prospect.

No Absolute Rules

The techniques suggested here are not hard and fast rules that apply to every brushdown attempt. In some instances an executive may tell you a subordinate does not have a clear buying mandate and yet that executive will make decisions based on recommendations from below. And in any one instance the right thing for you to do may be to present to the lower level.

For example, the top authority of a prospective account that has a large sales volume potential, one that is on your high-priority target list, insists that the only way you are going to get a chance for the company's business is to go through channels. Furthermore, she resists your persistent attempts at further probing. At least you tried your best to get Number One to take a look.

In another situation, you might be away from home base, in an area you're not likely to return to before a buying decision will be made, and you have no higher-priority prospects to call on in that vicinity at that time. In other words, it's now or never.

Stay with the Odds

But remember this matter of odds. They are not in your favor when a lower-level person does not have clear-cut authority. And if you repeatedly accept brushdowns, the law of averages will see to it that in the long run you'll be spinning your wheels, spending precious time presenting to and following up with people who do not have much influence in the buying decision. That time could be more profitably spent looking for a right person somewhere else. Besides, you are better off to avoid the emotional drain that goes with pursuing dead ends.

Make It Easy in the Long Run

Most important, realize that you will greatly improve your selling skill and consequent performance when you become more determined to hang in longer with higher-level buying authority. At least find out what the ground rules are so you know where you stand. Being quick to settle for lower authority may seem like taking the easier road at first, but the road will become more difficult along the way.

This Chapter in Perspective

This chapter states a central theme of this book: Getting a top-level decision maker to hear your presentation firsthand is in itself a sale to be made. The ability to do so is a paramount selling skill. Regardless of the range of your sales experience, you now have this ability to some degree. It is crucial for you to realize the importance of committing yourself to a never-ending quest to improve this skill.

Although the words you use in your dialog with a top authority are important, the quest cannot begin and end with just the words. The complete skill lies in understanding and putting into practice all the principles covered in this book.

13

Receptionists and Secretaries

Your First Contact—The Receptionist

The persons with the right buying authority that you are determined to meet are not to be found in the outer lobby waiting for your call. They are most often tucked away in an inner sanctum. Your first contact either in person or by phone with a business firm, nonprofit institution, or government unit will be a receptionist.

Chapter 15 will deal with telephone techniques and will include dialog with receptionists and secretaries. For now let's concentrate on in-person calls, even though phone dialog with them in some respects is similar.

In the reception lobby you may find handout brochures with a message telling how welcome salespeople are and that they will be given every opportunity to tell their story. But that may be on the company's terms, which is the lowest level in a screening hierarchy. Receptionists and secretaries are often trained to protect busy executives from *avoidable* interviews with salespeople who would waste an executive's time.

On the other hand, receptionists and secretaries also are given responsibility to see to it that visitors who have something beneficial to offer their organization will be helped in every way possible to state their case to the company's best advantage.

If your objective is to reach an upper executive, you will often find that a receptionist tends to steer you in the direction of a lower-level screener. This type of receptionist may voluntarily do very little to help you get to the top-level buying authority and, if not treated properly, can do a great deal to keep you out.

How to Greet Receptionists

In order to elicit proper treatment, your attitude is important. You are not a time waster, you have ideas, information, experience, and expertise that will be valuable to the right persons in this organization whether they buy from you or not. Your manner is one of unhesitating confidence yet without pretense or cockiness. A big, warm, friendly smile will go a long way toward helping you feel self-confident as well as toward making a good impression with other people.

It seems terribly elementary to mention the importance of smiling to anyone in sales. It is one of those things that should go without saying. Yet the next time you sit in a reception lobby where other salespeople approach a receptionist, watch their faces. How seldom you will see a genuine, warm smile.

With some people a smile comes easily, naturally. Others need to work at it. I had to. I can remember many photos taken when I was sure there was a nice wide grin on my face. But when the prints came back, not so. If you've experienced the same phenomenon, better work on it.

Some years ago, miniature rubber troll dolls were a big fad. I remember business executives who kept them on their desks just for decoration. The troll's facial features were grotesquely ugly. But what endeared them to everybody was a smile that spread from one huge ear to the other.

Stay on Course Toward Your Objective

It is best to tell a receptionist as little as possible without being deceptive and without making it obvious you want to tell as little as possible. This may seem contrary to today's trend toward openness. But there are times when it is to everyone's benefit to be less open. This is such a time. You want to avoid getting off to a wrong start with the wrong person and avoid the wasted time and frustration that is caused by taking such a direction at this stage.

You have a strategy for setting a course of action that will enable you to make the most effective use of everybody's time in serving the needs of prospective clients. You are rendering them a great service in taking pains to set it up right. Receptionists may not understand this. It is not your job to teach them to understand it. Therefore, you have little choice but to maintain a careful balance between reserve and openness. To do otherwise is to risk walking into the passageway that leads to an egress. You want to avoid having the receptionist decide the nature of your business and making some wrong assumptions about whom you should see.

To readers who call on buyers who are readily accessible, it may sound like I'm overdoing this business of being extra careful in getting to the right person. These techniques for them may not be necessary. I beg your forbearance and ask you to take from this book what applies to you.

When You Don't Know the Name

When approaching a receptionist, it is helpful to know the name of the person you want to see. But in case you don't know the name, don't let that stop you from making a call. Let's say your objective is to arrange an appointment with the president of a company and you don't know the name. Here is an approach to take:

You:	Good morning. I'd like to speak to the president of your company. Who would that be, please?
Receptionist:	Thomas Jackson.
You:	Would you please tell Mr. Jackson [your name] from [your company] is here to see him.
Receptionist:	What is this in regard to?
You:	The purpose of my call is to meet Mr. Jackson, state my business, and arrange an appointment. Would you please tell him that [your name] is here to see him.

Another approach when the name of the person you want to call on is not known is to ask an unusual question about that person. Let's say this time you want the top financial executive. You don't even know the title. It could be vice-president of finance, comptroller, controller, treasurer, manager of accounting, or whatever.

You:	I have a question.
Receptionist:	OK, what is it?
You:	Is your chief financial executive a man or a woman?
Receptionist:	A woman.
You:	What is her name?
Receptionist:	Betty Ross.
You:	Would you please tell Ms. Ross that *[your name]* from *[your company]* is here to see her.

The essence of this technique is to ask simple, closed-end questions that are easy for the receptionist to answer. This will help you maintain the initiative, get information you need, and lead you to your objective. In the preceding example you ordinarily wouldn't need to know Ms. Ross's title at this stage. You can find that out later. Avoid asking any more questions than necessary when there is a risk of being sent to a wrong person. When that risk is not present, feel free to get as much information as you can from a receptionist.

When You Do Know the Name

When you know the name of the person you want to see, your approach would be: "Good morning. Would you please tell Ms. Betty Ross that *[your name]* from *[your company]* is here to see her." This has a sound of positive expectancy. Even though you don't have an appointment and you are not saying that you do, this approach will call for higher regard from a receptionist than if you start out with, "Is Betty Ross in?"

"What Is This in Regard to?"

These approaches will usually get you directly to the person you want to see or to his or her secretary. Sometimes a question will be relayed to the receptionist, "What is this in regard to?" Don't try to give your opener to be relayed back. Instead say: "The purpose of my call is to meet Ms. Ross, state my business, and arrange an appointment." Sometimes you will get relayed back, "But what is your business?"

Simply ask, "Could I please state it directly to Ms. Ross?"

Keep your response in the form of a simple question. It is unlikely anyone would say no to that. The receptionist may ask you to pick up a lobby phone. Ms. Ross is on the line. Your request for direct contact is being honored. Go ahead now and state your opener over the phone. Don't press for face-to-face contact until after you give your opening benefit.

Sometimes Ms. Ross's secretary will either come out to meet you in the lobby or be on the line when you pick up the lobby phone.

How to Greet Secretaries

Secretaries, or executive assistants as they are often called, usually require different dialog than receptionists. Whereas a receptionist's responsibility is directing calls to everyone in the organization, secretaries are specifically concerned with one or very few individuals. They tend to be more skilled in the art of tactfully keeping unknown quantities out of their boss's office. Unconvinced of the importance of your mission, they will keep you out. On the other hand, when they believe you have something that will benefit their organization, they become an invaluable ally. The higher you go in an organizational hierarchy, the smarter and more powerful secretaries will be. Any hint of arrogance, tactlessness, or manipulation on your part is going to hurt your cause.

Secretaries tend to be adept and determined at getting the essential details of why you want to see the boss. The more information they get, the better they are doing their job. Your task is to give them enough information to justify recommending you for an interview. At the same time, avoid giving them any reason to make assumptions about your proposal that could curtail an opportunity to make a sale or get you shunted off to a screener.

Let's go back to the example in which your objective is to arrange an appointment with the president of a company. You get through your dialog with the receptionist. A woman comes out to the reception desk and says, "I am Linda, Mr. Jackson's assistant. What can I do for you?" Continue with:

> My name is_____from_____. The special reason for my
> visit here this morning is to meet Mr. Jackson, state my business
> to him, and arrange an appointment. Could we do that now?

She may usher you into Jackson's office without any special comment. But more likely she will ask a question such as: "What is this in regard to?" Your reply should be something like this:

> We are working closely with many companies similar to yours,
> with an idea that our clients tell us substantially cuts their
> operating costs. Mr. Jackson could quickly determine whether or
> not your company would want to consider this idea. Could I meet
> him now, or would one o'clock this afternoon be better?

This is the time to use general rather than specific benefits. And since it is the president of the company you want to speak with, use words that reflect a broad area of concern that is the domain of a president such as *operating cost* or *operational policy*. If instead, you were to use the words *cut manufacturing costs*, Linda would probably direct you to someone in manufacturing. That person may eventually turn out to be the right one, but you don't know that yet. At this point, your objective by an earlier decision is the president.

Add Urgency!

When there is a reason for urgency to your request for an immediate contact, be sure to emphasize it. There may be a limited offer or an impending price change. When you are working out of town, mention where you are from and the fact that now, while you are here, is the best, maybe the only opportunity for your prospect to learn about your idea. This is not the same as saying, "I just happened to be in the neighborhood."

Secretaries and Referrals

Here is an approach to a secretary using a referral. After your introduction say:

> My special reason for calling on Mr. Jackson is at the suggestion of
> one of his business associates who is a customer of ours. He felt
> certain Mr. Jackson would find a profitable application to a unique

idea we've developed. Would you please tell Mr. Jackson that I'm here.

Notice that the referrer's name was not given. Omitting the name here adds an extra touch to arouse Mr. Jackson's curiosity. Besides, the name is not likely to mean anything to the secretary.

When Pressed for More Information

If she presses for more information continue with:

I appreciate your question, but I have no way of telling you all about it in just a few words. I know from past experience that after discussing this with Mr. Jackson for a few minutes he will be able to judge whether or not he wants to give it further consideration. I'd be obliged if you could arrange to fit me into his schedule sometime today or tomorrow. Or if you can't make the appointment yourself, I'd be most appreciative if I could speak with Mr. Jackson for a minute right now and arrange the appointment with him personally.

Or try this variation:

I honestly don't know whether I could have any business with your firm or not. But one thing I'm quite sure of: Mr. Jackson will know in just a few minutes. If it's something that is of interest to him, I'll arrange a future appointment. But if it isn't, he'll tell me very quickly and we'll both save time.

The manner in which this kind of response is delivered is all-important. It should be like a sudden burst of sincerity that comes out of your mouth almost unexpected.

When an assistant absolutely refuses to let you in unless you give a detailed explanation and you are out in the reception lobby, first ask to go into his or her office. Once seated there say something like this:

First of all, we want to determine whether or not our idea would have a profitable application here. Would you mind if I get some answers to a few questions?

Then begin your probing for a need as was suggested in Chapter 11. Treat this person as though he or she were Number One. The typical secretary or assistant would not go through this without having some clout in an organization. An assistant could be in the process of being groomed for bigger responsibilities or in a smaller company could be in the family of the owner or a partner. A good up-front question in your probing would be aimed at finding that out.

Remember the Egress

Another frequent possibility is that an assistant will refer you to someone other than the person who was your primary objective. Before you accept that invitation, do some preliminary probing with the assistant to find out just how buying decisions are made in the organization.

The one you're being referred to may be the right person after all. Or if not, give yourself a chance to decide whether or not you are about to walk into an egress, what your odds are, and what course you may want to take. If it's a now-or-never situation, you may decide to go for it. If it's not urgent, another day, another approach may put you on more solid ground.

Ms., Miss, or Mrs.

A perplexing question that is often in the mind of male sales reps is, "How do you greet the feminist-era woman?" Some women still don't like the title Ms. prefixed to their name and probably never will. So when you hear a name like Betty Ross, what do you call her?

A "by the way" parting question to the receptionist can clear it up. When you are faced with a woman and don't know her preference, the advice I get from a consensus of women I polled is to use Ms. If she has a strong preference for Miss or Mrs., she will usually correct you and that's that. Whatever you do, don't make a big deal out of it.

Using Ms. as a prefix to a last name is certainly preferable to opting to use the first name with a total stranger in a business situation. The exception is when someone introduces herself with a first name only, as Linda did in the earlier example. This is a clear indication of the way she prefers to be addressed.

Heed Your Body Language

I've been suggesting words for you to use and, of course, the words are important, but the nonverbal aspect of your communication can make or break the words.

In addition to the smile we considered earlier, eye contact is another must. We think of our eyes as a sensing organ and, of course, they are. But they are more than that. Your eyes can talk even though their language is silent. When they are shifting around, they are announcing a shifty character. An alarm sounds with your host saying, "Proceed with caution."

When eyes can meet another person's with sincerity and warmth, they are saying, "Here is a sincere and friendly person worth trusting."

In the prefeminist days, men were to wait until a woman initiated a handshake. That is definitely out! Now either sex can be first to extend a hand in greeting.

Heed Your Style

There will be times when receptionists or secretaries are new on the job. Or things aren't going too well that day, or for some reason they feel anxious and emotionally vulnerable. Be alert for signs of this. Concentrate your first effort on helping them feel at ease.

Franklin Delano Roosevelt once said, "Everybody on earth is shy, self-conscious, and unsure of themselves. Everybody is timid about meeting strangers. So if you will just spend the first minute you are in the presence of strangers helping them feel comfortable, you will never suffer from self-consciousness again."

There is an often told but beautiful line attributed to an old Indian woman who once said, "I like me best when I'm with you." Help people to like themselves. Put them at ease with you. Forget about yourself and any self-conscious feeling you may have. Concentrate on the other person's feelings. He or she will be grateful and return your considerateness. Then you will feel much more self-confident.

And that's exactly the way you want to feel. A poised, confident manner that radiates complete belief in the words being said regarding benefits to the host organization will be the single most important factor in getting the right door opened. Consider that here is the ever-present question in a secretary's mind: "Is this stranger going to be a pestering time waster for the boss or a bearer of important information we can't afford to miss?"

Have an Ally, Not a Buffer

Know that secretaries are dedicated to the welfare of their bosses. They know the moods, whims, preferences, urgencies, and timing that will play an important bearing on the reception you will eventually get from your intended prospect. They quickly sense whether they are being regarded as an obstacle or an ally and will reflect your attitude toward them.

If you see a buffer, if you show impatience or irritation with the question, "What is this in regard to?" you're going to get a buffer who calls the shots at this stage and who knows how to give you a brushoff with ease. The same is true if you come on cocky, standoffish, patronizing, or overbearing, or if you come on wishy-washy, indecisive, weasel-worded, or over-anxious.

But if you see an ally, who is more concerned than you are to see that the boss gets important information, and if you treat this ally with all the courtesy, dignity, and unaffected warmth a good ally deserves, a good ally is what you will get.

The Inevitable Waiting

Cooling the heels in a reception lobby is an unavoidable way of life for most in-person sales reps calling on business firms. The perennial question is, How long should you wait? Some claim nice, easy answers to that and say, "Never more than 15 or 20 minutes," or whatever specific limit they choose to set. That may be OK for a general rule but some variables dictate that flexibility is wiser.

It is one thing when you have paid hundreds of dollars and hours of time traveling to get a key, target prospect, or when you have word that the prospect is in process of making a buying decision on what you sell. It is quite another when the call is in an area you frequent and there is no reason to believe a critical purchasing decision is imminent. Good judgment is the best rule.

Be a Watchful Waiter

When you are in a waiting situation, don't get yourself too comfortable in a deep-piled reception room chair engrossed with your favorite magazine. Rather, get into the habit of knowing what is going on at the reception desk without making a pest of yourself. All too many callers have missed opportunities to see a buyer because a receptionist was under the pressure of handling more messages than was humanly possible, was distracted, misplaced a note, was careless, or because there was a changing of the guard. Realize too, that receptionists, mortals that they are, are prone to all such misadventures in the pressure-cooker atmosphere of the reception room. Be understanding of the times when it is happening, yet tactfully be understanding of the progress being made with your mission. You have every right to know.

14

Fine-Tuning Your Call

A Prospect Under Pressure

Ward Bergquist is a media buyer for Advance Advertising Agency. Word is out that Advance has a big budget for print from one of its clients. Ward is besieged with reps calling on him and is beginning to feel a great deal of pressure as he is getting behind schedule. Most of the reps are from publications whose demographics only marginally fit the strategy Advance's creative staff had planned for their client. To make matters worse, the reps take up a lot of time with small talk.

Ward's office walls are covered with awards the agency has won, along with framed reprints of award-winning ads. Rep after rep would scrutinize them oohing and aahing, thinking that this was the way to make points. But while this is going on, Ward is only fuming. Long ago he wanted to get rid of the decorations but the president of the agency insisted on keeping them to impress clients and potential clients being solicited. To stop this intolerable waste of time, Ward told the receptionist that he would meet all reps in the lobby and conduct his business out there.

Brent Douglas represents a fairly new magazine whose demographics are perfect for the Advance client. This magazine's circulation got off to an amazing start and its editors were planning a theme for an upcoming issue that would tie in to the ad campaign. Brent had a good presentation to tell this story with a flip chart and beautifully prepared and compelling visual proof.

When he came to call on Advance, Ward quickly motioned for him to sit down in a reception lobby chair with shoulder-high sides. Ward sat in a similar chair next to him. The seats seemed to sink down almost to the floor. The chair sides were like a wall between them. The lobby was busy with phones ringing, other reps coming and going. Then a grade school class came through on a tour of "The World at Work."

Brent's presentation was a disaster! He missed an opportunity for a sale that should have been made. Ward Bergquist missed out on an excellent buy for his client.

Get the Proper Setting

The notion of setting up an appointment for a presentation on the right basis was mentioned several times in this book so far. The preceding little vignette illustrates what can happen when you don't take the initiative to do so. You work under a serious if not impossible handicap when the setting is not appropriate.

To proceed beyond the opener at an office rail or a doorway or in any circumstances which are uncomfortable for you or the prospect is asking for a washout. It is hopeless to attempt to present visual material in a stand-up presentation or in a situation like the one Brent Douglas found himself in. You are up to bat and the pitcher is throwing pitches that are impossible to hit. Reception lobbies with all their distractions, including other salespeople looking over your shoulder as you present, are likewise a poor setting. The only reason ever to use a lobby would be if any other alternative is less favorable—if, for example, your prospect's office or work area was a more distracting place.

It's not unusual for a prospect to invite you to sit down in a reception lobby and expect you to complete your call there. While it may be all right to state your opener out there, it is not wise to go beyond it without taking the initiative to suggest a better setting. Your proposition is too important to risk anything but the best. Believe that! When you neglect to ask for a better setting, you are nonverbally suggesting that what you have to offer is so casual that it is compatible with a casual setting.

When you suggest moving to a more appropriate place, include in your reason for doing so a benefit to the prospect. Point out that it can be given in less time or that visual and demonstration material are better seen at a desk or on top of some kind of display space. If the prospect's office is occupied or is a distraction, try for a conference room or any other place with some privacy. If the prospect's reason for denying use of the inner office is the pressure of a heavy workload or the presence of visitors with whom the prospect will be tied up for a while, you are better off to schedule an appointment for another time. Under these circumstances you're not likely to get proper attention anyway.

You Don't Need a Crutch

The sorriest reception lobby scenario is one I've seen often enough to realize it needs to be mentioned here. It goes like this: A prospect comes out to the lobby. In one of the sales rep's extended hands is a stack of note pads with the company's logo. In the other are some brochures. "I thought you might have some use for these note pads. And here is some literature about our products. If you ever need any or if you ever want some more information, give me a call, Uh, here is my card."

Incredible? It happens. If you've spent a fair amount of time in a reception lobby, you know it does. Don't you wonder what gets written on a daily report after a call like that?

Note pads with a logo are excellent for remembrance advertising. In most cases, brochures or catalog sheets or other kinds of literature are a must. I recommend to my clients' sales managers that they know how such sales aids are being used. Note pads, when used, are to be given out at the end of a presentation. Literature may be part of the visual material used in a presentation, but even better as a leave-behind. It's best for sales managers not to give note pads to trainees until they are sure to be used properly.

Giveaways are a holdover from days gone by when door-to-door selling was more prevalent. They were called door openers and were a good idea, because residential prospects are often more wary of strangers coming to call. Door openers are not necessary in the business world. To professional buyers and executives, calls by salespeople are daily routine, and door-opening gifts suggest you don't have much else going for you. Besides, they don't want to feel obligated. Your best door opener is an idea that offers a benefit.

Another crutch that prevails in selling is the misguided notion that the way to build rapport with someone is to select an outstanding feature on display, such as a trophy, a picture, or an indication of a hobby, and use that as a warm-up conversation starter.

How to Build Rapport

While it's true that some people you call on will enjoy or at least tolerate such small talk, in the busy business and professional world, it's a serious mistake to assume that everybody does. In fact, most do not, especially with strangers, when they are pressed for time, when they suspect that you are really not that enthusiastic about their special interest and you are only showing interest for effect. Your odds are always in favor of getting right down to the business at hand. Again, your best warm-up is a hot idea that offers a nice warm benefit. Then suggest or probe for ways your prospect can realize there is a need for the benefit and how that need can be satisfied. Even when you have someone who likes small talk, you are using up precious time with it. If the prospect is on a tight schedule the time could run out before you have a chance to complete your agenda.

The Right Kind of Enthusiasm

One of my clients, who is based in Dallas, told me this story:

I like to get to the office about a half-hour before office hours begin, have a cup of coffee, and read the morning paper. A rep who sells materials-handling equipment learned of my habit and came to pay me a call during my quiet time one Monday morning. This was OK with me as we were thinking about upgrading our equipment and I admire ambition in sales reps. I like to think our salespeople are doing the same.

As he walked into my office he noticed I had my paper open to the sports page. The Cowboys won a game in the last few seconds the day before so he latched on to this subject supposedly to provide a warm-up to his presentation.

And a good subject, too, because I'm a great Cowboy fan. His enthusiasm for Coach Landry and the team was unrestrained. It was almost as though he were in the stands himself cheering that winning two-minute drill, and he had me right there along with him. The Cowboys are the greatest. No argument from me about that.

Then we got down to business. What a letdown! When he opened his portfolio and started elaborating on his equipment, it was as if he shifted some internal gear. Oh yes, he was enthusiastic. But it was an obviously phony, contrived enthusiasm in stark contrast to the genuine enthusiasm he showed for the Cowboys. Well, we didn't buy from him, and I don't expect we will in the foreseeable future.

This rep was performing with two often misunderstood aspects of traditional sales lore. The first is, "Sell yourself first and your product second." This principle is valid, but be sure you sell your product with the same kind of enthusiasm as you sell yourself.

The second has to do with just what enthusiasm really is. Genuine enthusiasm must be based on genuine belief. You cannot separate the two. Enthusiasm is the verbal and physical expression of your belief in what you are selling. To act out enthusiasm is good for you to do by yourself when you are getting started in the morning or when you are feeling sluggish. It will help to perk you up. It's like an athlete's warm-up exercises. But putting on an act in front of a potential buyer in an opener situation is like telling the prospect to proceed with caution.

Be Yourself

Be yourself! This is such simple-sounding advice given to salespeople from an untold number of mentors—so simple-sounding that it seems it should be the easiest thing in the world to do. What could be more effortless than to just relax and do what comes naturally? But what a paradox when so often it doesn't turn out that way. For example, I was having breakfast with a sales rep I was to work with one day. Let's call him Bob. At breakfast Bob was the most pleasant, interesting, easy-going chap. But later when faced with a prospect, Bob seemed to shift a gear and become someone else—a person who looks and sounds different from the one with whom I had breakfast. Bob became what he thinks a salesperson should look and sound like. Unfortunately, in acting out this role, Bob hides Bob, the nice guy I enjoyed chatting with at breakfast.

The Pinnacle of Professionalism

A common denominator in such contrived behavior is tenseness. The opposite of tenseness is relaxation. To be yourself you must be relaxed. To be relaxed is first and foremost a physical thing. Like any physical skill it can be learned. While it is beyond the scope of this book to detail relaxation techniques, I suggest you consult your local public library or bookstore, where you will find many excellent books available on the subject. I would recommend *You Must Relax* by Edmund Jacobson, *Release from Nervous Tension* by David Harold Fink, and *The Relaxation Response* by Herbert Benson and Miriam Z. Klipper. These books offer specific techniques you can easily learn that will help you to be more relaxed, not only in selling situations, but in all areas of your life.

There is usually some degree of tension in the air, originating from both the prospect and the salesperson when they meet for the first time. It is part of your professional skill to know how to reduce any negative effect this tension may cause and to take the initiative to apply your mastery. Such skill begins with your ability to relax yourself. It would be impossible to bring it off without that ability.

Then too, be aware that regardless of the importance you may place on a call, it is just another incident in your prospect's long list of daily business contacts and routine. So relax and banish any thought that this or any other call will have a perilous or climactic influence on your sales career. Know in your heart that what you have to offer will be of benefit to your prospect. The best way to communicate that belief is in your own relaxed attitude of confident enthusiasm. Much persuasive power lies in a friendly, relaxed manner of greeting. It will do more than words to encourage a positive, open-minded response.

A relaxed attitude of confident enthusiasm will also suggest that you are no threat to ego, time, or budget and that you are big enough to accept the prospect's final decision, whatever it may be.

Do's and Don'ts to Fine-Tune Your Opener

DO

Relax.
Be yourself.
Smile.
Maintain eye contact.
Be confident.
Be friendly but not over-familiar.
Be positive, but gentle.
Let your belief show.
Show pride in your offering.
Be sure you've got the right buying authority.
Be flexible.

Maintain the initiative.
Offer a benefit.
Be brief.
Show genuine interest in your prospect.
Remember your objective.
Ask for an appointment.
Show respect for the prospect's time.
Be prepared for resistance.
Request sufficient time for your presentation.

DON'T

Be cocky.
Be apologetic.
Be demanding.
Be evasive.
Be shifty with your eyes.
Disguise the fact you have something to sell.
Be pushy.
Be hurried into an abbreviated or stand-up presentation.
Get angry or upset.

Get drawn into an argument.
Sound like a sixth grader reciting in class.
Get defensive.
Be too polished.
Use manipulative tricks.
Plead like a beggar.
Exaggerate.
Try to sell your whole story in the opener.

15

Sharpening Your Telephone Skills

Telephone, So What?

Can you imagine life without a telephone? Using the phone is such a familiar, everyday routine in our society. We've all been using it since we began to talk. What would anyone need to learn about using this simple instrument?

But the telephone has become so familiar that we take it too much for granted. We ordinarily use it without a second thought to any necessary technique. That may be all right for everyday routine calls. But to be effective in catching the attention and interest of preoccupied strangers requires planning, strategy, and discipline.

The Difference in Telephoning

Most of the basic methods of in-person openers dealt with so far apply on the telephone as well. The difference in approach has to do with three main considerations. First of all, the spoken word and along with it, the quality, speed, and tone of voice take on a new measure of importance. Second, neither you nor the prospect can see what is going on. You lose the communicative impact of body language, and you lose the opportunity to gather information from any other physical signs. And third, there are particular stresses commonly associated with sustained telephone use for which you must be prepared. There is a much faster pace to telephone contact. Rejection comes quicker. Its cumulative effect takes a heavier emotional toll on most salespeople. Mobility and change of pace afforded by traveling from one call to another aren't there. Of course, this last item is a concern during sustained phone activity, not for an occasional call.

Telephone Call Objectives

Some products and services can be presented and sales closed over the telephone. These would include items whose grade qualities are easily described such as commodities, repeat items that buyers are familiar with, and special offers such as price reduction or any extra benefit that can be offered on a temporary basis.

With products that require a personal call to close a sale, the telephone can be used to gather information, qualify prospects, and make appointments. It is important to establish your objective before each call. Decide just exactly what you want to happen.

Develop a Pleasing Voice

Regardless of the objective of a phone call, your voice is a predominant factor that will help you or hurt you. Let's zero in on it. A friendly conversational tone is fundamental. If your natural speaking style is too fast, too slow, too loud, too soft, slurred, or otherwise out of step with the person on the other end of the line, you will need to make a special effort to modify it. Your friends may be tolerant of such imperfections, but don't expect prospects to be.

By special effort, I mean it may take some work to form new habits of speech so the speech patterns will sound natural, not contrived. Here again, a tape recorder can be a valuable tool. As you listen to the playback, imagine you are the prospect listening to unknown words coming from the voice of a total stranger. Ask yourself these questions: Is it easy to listen to? Is it easy to understand? We are usually not completely objective in evaluating our own voice. Better to get coaching from your supervisor, an

experienced salesperson, or someone whose evaluation you will
have confidence in.

Mind Your Speed and Pitch

Most people will feel comfortable listening to you at a speaking
rate of 140 words per minute. To determine this speed, read a
prepared text containing 700 words and time it. It should take five
minutes to average the desired speed. If your normal rate is faster
or slower, practice until you get a feel for the 140-word rate. It is
important, however, to keep in step with the person you are
speaking with. If they speak slower, slow your rate down. If they
give indication of a hearing problem, speak a little louder. If they
speak faster, speed up. Fast-talking prospects can easily become
impatient with slow-talking salespeople, while slower-talking ones
become suspicious of fast talkers.

Actually, 140 words per minute is somewhat slower than most
people naturally speak. But the telephone tends to accentuate
speed. It usually sounds faster to the person listening than it really
is. People tend to tune out fast-talking strangers on the phone.
Sloppy, slurred diction is common in our society today. Since the
voice predominates and body language is absent, poor diction
stands out all the more on the phone. It is uncomfortable to listen to
someone who is difficult to understand. The natural tendency for a
prospect who feels uncomfortable listening to a difficult-to-under-
stand salesperson is to terminate the conversation as quickly as
possible. Any excuse will do as long as it serves to get rid of the
uncomfortable feeling, even though what is being said would be
beneficial. Yet the same salesperson having favorable, compensating
personality characteristics would get by with poor diction in person.
All the more reason to heed your telephone diction.

Check the pitch of your voice. Is it too high? If so, take any
object from your desk, such as a pen or a piece of paper, and put it
on your lap. Look at it as you talk and pitch your voice at it. The
pitch of your voice will move downward. A lowered voice sounds
warmer and more friendly.

Practice using your friendly telephone sales personality whenever you pick up the phone, not just when talking to prospects. For example, how do you talk to salespeople who call you on the phone? How about your children's friends, people below you in status, people you don't particularly like? To acquire the habit of a pleasing, friendly telephone voice, it is important to use it at all times instead of practicing a double standard.

Confidence—The Most Important Quality

Warmth and friendliness are desirable voice qualities, but this does not mean you should sound subservient in any way. In fact, the most important quality is the sound of confidence grounded in a deep conviction that you know what you are talking about and that you believe it will benefit the prospect. The more genuine the certainty in your voice, the more likely the prospect will want to hear you out.

Let me repeat something that was written in an earlier chapter: *It is imperative that you see yourself as a competent, knowledgeable expert in your field and that you have information and ideas that will be of benefit to your prospects.*

The practical application of this image of yourself at the point of contact with a prospect is the single most powerful, compelling, persuasive force when using the telephone. To fail to understand its importance is to fail to open doors of selling opportunity. Remember your positive affirmations. Repeat them as part of your precall preparation. Repeat them whenever you feel your confidence slipping.

Use a Script

Prospects are prone to make the decision of whether or not to allow a conversation to continue quicker on the phone than in a face-to-face opener. They permit interruptions in the middle of tasks for which they would not in a face-to-face call. Granted, that choice of words is critical in a face-to-face call, and it is even more so on the phone. An important advantage of using a phone, therefore, is that you can use a script. But remember to compose the script using the suggestions in Chapter 10 for composing the words to an in-person opener. It should be spoken, rather than written language. Practice it until it sounds conversational.

A key question is, does your script sound like you? A third-party advisor is an invaluable aid. A tape recorder is a must. Make liberal use of marginal and parenthetical notes on your script regarding inflections, emphasis, pauses, and other nonverbal signals. Then practice and listen to your tape-recorded playback until you deliver it effortlessly with a natural, spoken sound. At some point, from repetitive use, you will probably have the script memorized. Nevertheless, keep it in front of you when calling. It frees your mind to make other observations and to plan how to proceed.

The content of a telephone script will depend on the objective of the call. Sales of some products and services are closed over the phone by relatively inexperienced salespeople reading scripts prepared for them. No doubt you've listened to this type of approach. It is commonly referred to as a boiler room operation. Techniques of such operations are not dealt with in this book.

The emphasis in this chapter is on making initial telephone contact with selected business prospects for the purpose of gathering information, qualifying the prospects, identifying needs, and making appointments to call on qualified prospects.

How to Get Information

Some of the information gathering can be done before you get to the right person you eventually want to reach. It is easier to get relevant information from subordinates by phone than in person. They don't know who you are. You could be a customer seeking information or someone else within their company. If the person you have on the line can't tell you what you want to know, ask for someone who can. When you don't know the name of the person you want, use dialog similar to that suggested in Chapter 13. By phone, it's easier to get through to those who can give you information and you avoid starting off on the wrong foot with the wrong person. Just as it is easier for prospects to terminate a contact on the phone, the same goes for you. Use that to your advantage when it is wise to do so. Often it is better to hang up, courteously, of course, when you get the information you want and call back another time to get through to the right person. Then there will be more certainty in your approach, and you're less likely to get sidetracked.

Getting to the Right Person

OK. You have enough preliminary information, including the name of the person you want. Let's say it's James Madison. You dial the number. The phone rings and someone answers with, "Good morning, Madison Company."

You don't know who answered. It could be Mr. Madison. It could be a receptionist, secretary, or just anybody who happened to pick up the phone. Regardless, the first thing you say is:

"Mr. Madison, please."

Notice there is no question mark at the end of that statement. It's a statement, so it shouldn't sound like a question. The most common opening line salespeople use on the phone goes something like this, "Is Mr. Madison in?" That sounds like you don't know much about the comings and goings of Mr. Madison. Making it a statement instead will prompt fewer chances of being asked questions about the nature of your business, fewer chances of getting sidetracked.

Now the person who answered the phone may ask you to identify yourself, which you do by merely giving your name. You may then be asked to identify your company, which you do by giving the name of your firm. Take note that at this point you are giving only the information for which you are asked. After you give your name and again after you identify your company, say without pausing, "May I speak with Mr. Madison, please." You may get a third request that takes the form of, "May I tell Mr. Madison what this is about?"

Let's say your objective is to speak directly with Mr. Madison to qualify him as a prospect or get some information regarding his needs before you decide whether or not you want to make an appointment with him at this time. When asked the nature of your call by the person that answered the phone, say something like this:

"The purpose of my call is to find out if our company would have any business with Mr. Madison. May I speak with Mr. Madison, please."

When your objective is to get an appointment, reply with: "The purpose of my call is to introduce myself to Mr. Madison, state my business, and arrange an appointment. May I speak with Mr. Madison, please."

In most cases this would get you through to him or to his secretary or executive assistant, who would probably say, "Mr. Madison's office." You reply: "Mr. Madison please."

Once again this is a statement that should not take the tone of a question. And again, identify yourself and your company only when asked.

If the secretary asks about the nature of your call, your reply would be the same as to the first person who answered the phone: "The purpose of my call is to introduce myself to Mr. Madison, state my business, and arrange an appointment. May I speak with Mr. Madison, please."

Sometimes at this point you will get diverted to someone other than Mr. Madison. The secretary will say, "I'll let you speak with Mr. Monroe."

Be prepared to come back immediately, before the switch is made. Find out what Mr. Monroe's title is, what his position is in the company. Get as much information as you can about his decision-making credentials so you know where you stand.

When you are using a referral or you are asked for further clarification of the nature of your business, proceed along the same lines suggested in Chapter 13 for dialog with secretaries and assistants regarding those situations. Be sure to end each statement with, "May I speak with Mr. Madison, please."

Flexibility Requires Good Judgment

The techniques suggested here are not inflexible. There may be good reason why you would want to give more information to persons screening your call. You may be responding to an inquiry. There may be recognizable prestige to the organization you represent. You may have reason to believe that Mr. Madison would be especially interested in talking to you, or any one of many other considerations. Good judgment should prevail.

A receptionist or secretary may say that Mr. Madison is unavailable at the time you call. Then be sure to ask when he is likely to be available. If the reply is indefinite, inquire about his daily routine: what time he arrives in the morning, leaves at the end of the day, goes out to lunch. Some people get to their jobs very early in the morning or stay late in the evening. Some rarely go out to lunch. Some are in on Saturdays. These are times when busy executives are not as likely to be involved with other appointments.

Find out if your right person has a direct-line phone number. Using it will circumvent a switchboard and sometimes other screeners. Executives often answer their own phones even though they have assistants.

Whenever you are told that the person you want is busy, in a meeting, or otherwise unavailable, it is often possible to get him or her to come to the phone by being persistent. Such persistence is rarely wise. The only time it could be excused is when you are reasonably sure that person will consider the contact at least as important as you do and when your call has some kind of now-or-never urgency.

Person-to-person long-distance calls often get you directly to those hard to reach. It may be expensive when done frequently, but it can be cost-effective for high-potential prospects, especially when other attempts to reach them fail.

Should You Ask to Have Your Call Returned?

If you are unable to reach Mr. Madison at the time you place the call, you are most likely to be asked, "Is there a message you wish to leave for him?" You want to talk with him directly, so there isn't any intermediate message. What you are really being asked is, "Do you want Mr. Madison to return your call?"

Some people diligently return every phone call, others return only when they can identify the caller or have reason to believe the call is one they want to take.

If you are a typical salesperson, you don't spend much time sitting in the office with an open phone waiting for someone to call. You are either out making in-person calls or using your phone.

So generally speaking, it's better not to have calls returned by prospects. At least not until you've made several attempts at direct contact. But when the only way to get through to your right person is to have the call returned, then make arrangements for that.

Your Prospect Is on the Line

OK, now you have Mr. Madison on the line. Your opener to him will contain the same three parts as with an in-person opener, that is: (1) introduction of yourself and your company, (2) an opening benefit, and (3) a request for an appointment. But now we add a couple of optional requests, for a telephone interview or phone presentation if you intend to close sales on the phone.

Introductions take on special importance on the phone because he can't see you. Two questions are in his mind right from the start: Who is calling? And is it someone I'm supposed to know? You need to answer those questions quickly and clearly before you say anything else. Otherwise he may not listen to what you say. He will be distracted by searching for answers to those questions in his mind. This doesn't happen in person because then these questions are answered by sight.

If Mr. Madison answers with "Hello" or anything other than his name, you begin with, "Mr. Madison, please." Remember that is a statement, not a question. If he answers the first time with his name or responds to your first statement with yes or, "This is he," repeat his name but this time add his first name or initials and now make it sound like a question. When he responds again with yes, reply with, "Thank you." Repeat his name again, introduce yourself, and continue with the opener. The sequence would go like this:

Mr. M.: Hello.
You: Mr. Madison, please.
Mr. M.: This is he.
You: Mr. James Madison?
Mr. M.: Yes.

You: Thank you, Mr. Madison. My name is Pat Murphy with Acme Corporation. Mr. Madison, my company is serving many manufacturing firms with an idea that our customers find substantially reduces hours of labor on certain manufacturing processes. My special purpose in calling you today is to find out if it would have an application to your business. Would this be a good time to get your answers to a few questions?

Remember that people will often allow the telephone to interrupt tasks for which they would not allow interruptions on an in-person call. Therefore it is important to check their availability early on. Sometimes they will pick up the phone because they were expecting some other important call. When they find out it's you instead, that would not be a good time for you to continue. You want to find that out. And when you do, back off. Offer to call another time. Ask for a suggestion when it would be better to call.

Variations of the Script

The techniques covered in Chapter 11 for situations when you don't know the name of the right person—using referrals, benefit statements, qualifying, probing for needs, avoiding prejudgment, and closing for appointments—apply on the telephone as well. Refer to Chapter 11 when preparing your telephone script. Compose variations to suit your objective, whether it is to qualify a prospect, identify needs, arrange an appointment, or close a sale. Be sure to keep in the forefront of your mind the importance of an effective benefit statement. It is the key to your right to be heard. The first drafts of your script are not likely to be the final product. As you use a script you will discover better words to use, better approaches.

Editing the Script

When editing look for ways to simplify and keep it short. If you can establish a firm foundation of interest in 30 seconds with a strong benefit, you have a great advantage. Busy people will often honor a request for a half-minute on the phone. If the conversation goes beyond that, it's because they want to hear more. Tell them so up front.

Refine your script to cut out unnecessary words and phrases. Make sure your benefit stands out in bold relief. Cut out weasel words. Replace longer, hard-to-pronounce words with those that are shorter, easier to pronounce. Longer words have more possible meanings. If your prospect doesn't follow the meaning easily, interest is lost, and along with it a sales opportunity.

Do your editing by listening to the tape-recorded version. Ask yourself, does it sound like written or spoken language? Is the meaning clear? Avoid any stretch more than 15 seconds long. Break up longer stretches with questions. Have a separate script sheet with a variety of typical questions. Be prepared to use them for any contingency. After asking a question, shut up and listen.

Open-end questions are especially important on the phone. In face-to-face situations you have visual material, body language, and perhaps demonstrations to help sustain interest. None of this is there to work for you on the phone. Therefore, you need to make extra effort to get more active participation from prospects. Open-end questions will help you to do this. Review all of the questioning techniques learned in Chapter 8.

Setting Appointments

When your objective is to get an appointment, take the lead in suggesting times to get together. Don't hesitate on this point. Hesitation can mean missed opportunity. During an in-person opener you have the option of continuing with a spot interview or presentation. A parallel situation on the phone is to offer to come over right away if that is convenient for both parties. This is especially wise when the prospect has shown some initial resistance.

As you know, not all appointments hold up. Boyan's law states that, "The firmness of an appointment diminishes with the square of the time elapsed between the opener and the appointment date." The old saw "Strike while the iron is hot" fits here. The benefits you emphasized that lessened the prospect's reluctance tend to be quickly forgotten. The more time that has elapsed, the greater the chance that something will turn up in a prospect's world to compete with that time slot. The sooner you follow up with an appointment, the better.

When an appointment is set for another week it may be a good idea to reconfirm it. I say, may be, to suggest caution. On the one hand, Boyan's law takes effect and makes it seem wise to reconfirm. But on the other hand, another telephone contact with a prospect gives him or her an opportunity to beg off.

To lessen the chance of appointments becoming unglued, take some extra precautionary measures at the outset. When you get a verbal agreement on time and date say something like this: "Mr. Madison, I'm now writing down on my calendar 8:00 A.M. on May 6. Would you please do the same so we can both be sure to have it right? I have 8:00 A.M. on May 6, OK?"

When you call back to reconfirm, it's best to do it the day before the appointment is scheduled. It's best to have someone call for you or try to confirm it with a secretary. If you get Mr. Madison on the line instead, quickly come to the point, confirming time and place, and end the call politely but without unnecessary conversation. If he tries to beg off, be prepared to resell, coming out with benefits again. If that doesn't keep the original date firm, come right back with suggested alternative dates.

Another good way to help keep an appointment firm is to drop a note in the mail, a postcard will do, as a reminder. Lead off your message with a thank you and restate the benefit something like this: "Thank you, Mr. Madison, for agreeing to get together with me on May 6. I promise to leave you with several good ideas which our clients have found reduce their manufacturing costs. See you at 8:00 A.M. sharp."

Precall Letters

An effective technique that helps get the attention of hard-to-reach prospects is an introductory letter sent in advance of your first phone call. Keep the letter short, with a strong benefit written to arouse curiosity. For this reason it's best not to include any descriptive literature unless the product described is so revolutionary that, by itself, it would arouse curiosity. A brochure designed to arouse curiosity rather than describe a product, or a provocative article from a magazine that tells about a problem for which you have a solution would be good. Limit the size of what you send to fit a standard number ten envelope. It should look like a personal letter, that is, not junk mail. Enclosing your business card or stapling it to the letter is also a good idea.

A phone call to a secretary, in advance of your mailing, to find out whether or not the right person will be in when your letter and follow-up call come in will greatly increase your chances. Be sure you have the correct spelling of the person's name, also that of the company. Don't abbreviate unless that is the style they use. Some people take offense at little things like that.

Confine your mailings to high-priority or otherwise hard-to-reach prospects. Don't get hooked on precall letters. Some salespeople won't pick up the phone unless a letter went out first. They find things to do other than selling when they run out of premailed prospects to follow up. On the other hand, don't send out more mailings than you can follow up in a week. The effect of such letters wears off quickly.

Here is an example of a precall letter:

Dear_____:

Because of the undoubtedly heavy demands upon your time, I am taking this means to introduce my company and myself.

The enclosed article from *Business News Monthly* entitled "Are Your Employees Costing You Money . . . Or Making You Money?" dramatically points out how easily payroll dollars can be unnecessarily wasted. We are currently serving thousands of business firms with a simple and inexpensive supplement to management's efforts that our clients tell us has upgraded the performance of their people and reduced payroll costs substantially. I will contact you within the next few days for an appointment, at your convenience, so you may evaluate our idea in terms of profit to your organization.

When you follow up with your telephone opener, state the opener as you would had you not sent the letter. Lead with your benefit. Reminding a prospect that you sent a letter is not a good opening line. It is not a very compelling benefit. Don't use the letter as a crutch for something to say. A benefit is the most important thing you can say. Why start the game with your second string? It's better if the prospect mentions the letter first. If not, you can make reference to it and any supporting enclosure at a later point in the dialog.

Preparing for Extended Telephone Use

When using the phone regularly for long periods of time, give some attention to the physical setup of your surroundings. You can be at your best only when you're free of distraction and give the task a full measure of concentration, physically, mentally, and emotionally. Privacy and quiet are ideal, but not the case in every office. Do what you can to arrange for it.

Before you start calling, make sure everything you need is handy—writing materials, prospect files, scripts, appointment books, and anything else you find that makes the job go more smoothly. If you are right-handed, put the telephone to your left on the desk. Then your right hand will be free to take notes and the cord will be out of your way. For extended telephone use, some people prefer using a headset, sometimes called a star set. Then both hands are free to gesture, which helps you to speak more expressively, and to retrieve data from files. Star sets are available from the phone company or from electronics stores that sell phone equipment. If you don't have a push-button phone, get one. Granted, what you do to it is still called dialing.

In precall planning, express your objectives in terms of some end result, such as number of appointments made, number or total dollar volume of sales, number of prospects qualified. It is better to aim for these end results rather than expressing your objective as the amount of time spent on the phone.

Keep Dialing

Get your prospect cards stacked in advance. During the planning stage is the time to make decisions as to who you're going to call and in what order. Once you start calling, keep dialing one call after another until you've reached your goal or it's time to take a break. Schedule ten minutes of break time each hour. It's important to stay fresh.

Every call will not be productive, but some percentage will. Keep in mind, though, that every call contributes to the final goal. The law of averages is working. Even when several in a row are disappointing, you will have to get through those to uncover the productive ones. To that extent, those calls were successful. So keep dialing.

Keep a record of the number of calls you need to make, to produce a certain number of appointments, which results in so many dollars of sales or commission. Let's say it takes ten calls, including prospects who are unavailable, to get one appointment. You sell one out of three appointments for an average commission of $200.00. Then each call earns you $6.60 whether you reach a prospect or not. Think about that as you dial.

The bane of telephone success is the ease with which you can find things to do other than dialing the next number. Such things as rearranging prospect cards, talking with an associate, or stopping to figure out what is wrong. Usually nothing is wrong. It's just that the law of averages is giving you one kind of streak. It happens. The cumulative effect of repeated "not in," "too busy," "not interested," builds up much faster on the phone than in person. Be prepared to accept this as a fact of life. It would be nice if they were spread out evenly, but more likely they come in bunches. Your best bet to even things out is to keep dialing.

On the other hand, the time when you set an appointment or close a sale is the time you're best equipped physically, mentally, and emotionally to be effective. Now you've gained momentum. By continuing activity, the motivating power of momentum will go to work for you. This is not the time to let up. If you do, the force of constant activity upon which momentum depends is gone.

Record Information

When you have a prospect on the line, be sure to write down all the pertinent information you hear—things like when purchases are likely to be planned in the future, what needs were disclosed, names of buying influentials. Write down comments for which you may want clarification or feedback to the prospect later. When an appointment is made, confirm the address and get directions if you're not sure of the location.

If you need to have a variety of scripts depending on what the prospects' needs are and you don't know which one to have ready, here is an idea. Have each script on a separate sheet of paper and cut the sheets to varying lengths. Arrange them by length with the shortest piece on top. Put the title or identification of each sheet at the very bottom. As you look at this file only the top sheet and the titles of each page will show. It will then be easy to find the script you need.

The Other Side of Techniques

As you can see from this chapter, to be effective making approaches on the telephone requires a lot more than the casual attention we ordinarily give to using this commonplace instrument. In addition to learning the techniques, it takes energy and a positive mind-set. Good technique is the result of intelligent planning and the will to form sound habits. Execution is something else.

Fatigue, lack of sleep, hangovers, and a negative mental state can eradicate good technique. These are all factors which have a pronounced, conspicuous effect on the way your words sound to a prospect. And they are factors over which you have complete control. You choose to do or not to do what is necessary to be prepared physically and mentally. Your physical and mental state will determine how you feel emotionally. To choose behaviors that assure you are well rested and not hung over is obvious. And there is no deep, dark secret to maintaining a positive attitude. Suggestions for doing that are sprinkled throughout the pages of this book. Although these suggestions apply to all phases of selling, they most urgently need to be applied when using the phone.

It is as if we had a stereo tape recording in our head. One track has positive thoughts reminding us of all the wonderful benefits of what we sell and how our prospects will be happy we came along.

The other track is reminding us that people on the other end of the line are busy and resent being interrupted by pestering salespeople.

If we do not exercise conscious control of our thoughts, they will be influenced by exterior forces. When these forces are positive, they serve as a catalyst to propel us with positive energy. The volume is turned up on the positive stereo track.

But when these forces are negative, as they often are in selling, and they come faster, with greater intensity on the phone, up goes the negative volume, down goes the positive volume. Down goes our performance.

And when that happens, we must step in and take over the volume controls. In fact, the most successful salespeople form a habit of keeping their hands on the controls at all times.

16

Paraphrasing

The Value of Just One Idea

In this chapter you are going to learn *paraphrasing*, a technique that many salespeople tell me proved to be the most valuable addition to their sales skills repertory they ever learned—one that dramatically changed their status in the sales profession from just OK to top producers in an amazingly short time. The reason for their quantum leap to success came from a newly acquired ability to set up presentations under the best of circumstances with prospects who responded to an opener with indifference, yet had very important problems that needed to be solved.

The Meaning of Paraphrasing

To paraphrase in selling is to rephrase a prospect's statement with words that will reveal unexpressed meanings and feelings lying hidden beneath the original statement. These unexpressed meanings and feelings often give clues to a need. The paraphrase clarifies the language. It brings the need out into the open and gets the prospect to agree that it is a need.

You will find the technique is easy to learn if you have grasped the essence of Chapters 5 through 9. It has always been a source of wonder to me why I find so few salespeople who know about this powerful technique, let alone who use it to good effect. All too often high-priority prospects with real needs, wants, problems, and dissatisfactions are written off at their first expression of indifference. Yet these often turn out to be the best long-term customers. Competition for their time and attention is less because so few other salespeople get through to them. This technique can be used on the telephone as well as in person. Here is an example of the way it works:

Change "Too Busy" into "Better Find Time to Look"

One of my clients is a manufacturer of automated livestock feeding systems sold primarily to dairy farmers. These systems greatly reduce the labor a farmer must put forth to feed a herd. Tim Wall, a salesman for the company, recalled a dialog he had with a farmer on a new prospect call. Tim no sooner introduced himself and identified the company he represents than the farmer looked up from the machine he was repairing and declared, "Sorry, I'm not going to have time to talk to you. Just too much work to do around here."

"You've got a pretty big operation. Do you work it all by yourself?" Tim asks a closed-end question in order to learn an important fact.

"Yes."

"How do you manage to get all those chores done by yourself?" Tim probes further with an open-end question.

"I tell you, it's rough. My son went away to college this year so it's the first time I'm alone since we got so big. It's hard to find a dependable hired hand around here, so I guess I'll just do what I have to do."

"It seems to me you would like to figure out a way to cut down on some of these chores and still produce the same amount of milk. And that's what you really want, isn't it?" Tim paraphrased.

"Yes, I suppose so," the farmer agreed.

"That's great," Tim replied, "because my special reason for calling on you this morning is just to meet you and arrange an appointment for a time, at your convenience, when you can take a look at an idea that many dairymen find cuts their feeding chores in half. Could we do that this evening, or would tomorrow be better?"

When to Use a Paraphrase

In Chapter 8 it was suggested that the finest expression of tact in revealing your prospects' needs is to allow them to state a need in their own words. Rarely will someone come right out and in explicit, concise words articulate a need that can be satisfied by what you sell. More often you get bits and pieces or vague generalities that merely hint at possible needs. Sometimes you even hear an attempt to cover up a real problem.

Those bits, pieces, generalities, and coverups are signals for you to go on the alert. Focus your concentration on applying all the Chapter 9 listening skills. In particular, listen to identify feelings that lie hidden beneath the words you hear. Try to fill in the blank spaces of what is being omitted. The generalities are also a cue for using the questioning skills from Chapter 8 to reduce vague statements to something specific.

The situation Tim Wall faced is very common on a first call. A prospect is preoccupied with other matters and therefore indifferent to what a salesperson may want to discuss. The best way to change the attitude of indifference to one of interest is to ask questions until a need, a problem, or a dissatisfaction is uncovered.

Once a need is revealed, the next step is to suggest a benefit your product or service offers that will satisfy the need. Then if a complete presentation is necessary, suggest doing that on the spot if it is a personal call or set an appointment for a future presentation date.

How Background Information Helps Chart the Course

With most selling situations needs are fairly predictable. If you are selling a product like Tim's that offers the latest labor-saving technology and the prospect is using obsolete equipment, the need is probably obvious to you. If you are selling a financial service that offers tax breaks of which your prospect is not taking advantage, again, the need is obvious to you but perhaps not to the prospect.

It is helpful to get as much preliminary information about each prospect as possible. Tim Wall had the advantage of being on the scene of the problem. He could tell with his experienced eye that the ancient silo and obsolete equipment spelled "trouble in River City." When he found out that it was being worked by only one man, that meant even bigger trouble. Tim's objective, then, was to arrange a time when he could tell his whole labor-saving story under the most advantageous conditions.

Overlook Knee-Jerk Reactions

Tim had heard that "I don't have time to talk to you" routine many times before. He knew that kind of statement is just an unthinking reaction, not a firm position. Furthermore, he realized the best way to meet his objective was to get the prospect to feel that it was his own idea to take the time to listen.

Paraphrasing allowed Tim to clarify the language and so put the need in recognizable, concrete terms. Even though the farmer didn't choose the very words Tim used in his paraphrase, for all practical purposes he felt they were his. He in fact agreed that what Tim said is what he meant. His agreement was a perfect entrée for Tim to offer to show him an idea that would be worth taking the time to think about as a solution to his problem.

The comments you hear in the early phases of a contact with a new prospect that reflect indifference usually sound something like this:

"I'm not interested."

"I'm too busy to see you."

"I don't want to get into that now."

"We are satisfied with our present source of supply."

"Not going to spend any money now."

"Call me in a couple of months."

All too often, salespeople take these comments at face value, terminate the contact, and go look for another prospect. In other words, they are just out cherry picking.

Paraphrasing Cushions the Bluntness

Even when they do hang in there, a common mistake salespeople often make is to come back with a blunt question that has a blatantly obvious answer, which was advised against in Chapter 8, such as: "You do want to make more profit, don't you?" "You do want to cut your costs, don't you?" "You do want to safeguard your family's health, don't you?"

Questions like this are sure invitations to rejection. They are accusatory. Prospects become defensive about them. You get drawn into an argument you may win in logic, but you will lose an opportunity to make a sale.

It is contrary to human nature for anyone to suddenly switch from "I'm not interested," or any other such objection to "yes, I am interested and will listen to your presentation" on the basis of such blunt questions.

Paraphrasing allows the prospect a face-saving opportunity to make a more graceful change of mind. When Tim Wall used a paraphrase, it took more than a blunt question for the dairy farmer to switch from "Sorry, I'm not going to have time to talk to you" to agreeing it would be worth considering.

Besides being blunt, questions used in the examples four paragraphs ago are too abstract—too far removed from an immediate problem a prospect can "feel in the bones."

Get the Main Issue Up Front

In earlier chapters we considered things like empathy and how deep is the craving of people to be understood. The best kind of understanding takes place at levels of immediate, real-world experience—specific situations you can point to. It has often been said that people don't buy because they understand your product as much as they buy because they feel you understand them.

Paraphrasing gives you a vehicle to translate general statements into something specific that prospects can identify as being a problem of immediate concern. Thus, they are more likely to give it higher priority in addition to getting a stronger feeling that you understand them.

Realize, then, as Tim Wall did, that initial objections are not firm stands or even the main issue. The main issue is that you have something that will benefit your prospects—that will satisfy specific needs. To get this main issue to be the topic of conversation you must first isolate the need. Then you want your prospects to *agree* that they recognize it. Like the River City townfolk in *The Music Man*, they are singing along with you that there is "trouble in River City."

An Irresistible Invitation to Hear Your Story

Now they are in the best frame of mind to consider your solution. At this point of agreement, tell of a benefit that relates to the need you've identified and ask for an opportunity to make a full presentation.

When the dairy farmer agreed that it sure would be worth thinking about a way to cut down on some of his chores, Tim came right back with the suggestion that he had something which was proven to do just that. Then he asked for an appointment.

It is usually difficult and unlikely for anyone to refuse to hear your full presentation when a strong need is hanging out there in bold relief and an opportunity to take a look at a solution is being offered.

Persistence at Its Best

Sometimes after a paraphrase, a realization begins to dawn that the need you exposed is greater than the prospect was at first willing to admit. It can take some time for the full realization to sink in. All the while he may be hesitating to agree to an appointment, but still he can't give you a straight-out no. This is when it pays for you to hang in there. Especially in the case of a business need. For to ignore it is fraught with risk that could spell big trouble for a business prospect.

I hope we've laid to rest any reluctance to bring needs, problems, or dissatisfactions out into the open. The truth is, we do a great disservice to our clientele if we do not use our persuasive skills to help them find a better way.

Giving Prospects Valuable Perspective

Business people, especially, become so engrossed in the routine details of running their business, they often fail to see needs that are obvious to an outsider. There is an old saying, "Important things are put aside for the urgent until the important things become urgent and then sometimes it is too late." You can help people put things in their proper perspective, help them to take action on some important things before they become urgent.

Keep in mind that the purpose in paraphrasing is to bring out into the open unspoken needs, wants, problems, dissatisfactions. If a problem is stated directly by a prospect, there is no reason to paraphrase. In such a case simply tell of a benefit that relates to the problem and close the sale. Or on an initial contact when a complete presentation is necessary, ask for an opportunity to do so.

How to Start a Callback

When you set an appointment to make the presentation at a future date, be sure to begin the callback with a restatement of the need and again get an agreement. People quickly and easily forget.

Try this sometime: Ask people if they ever saw a visual aid that you showed on a previous call. Often they will have no recollection of having seen it before. Whatever you do, don't make an issue of the fact that they saw it before. Accept the reality of human forgetfulness and deliver that part of your presentation just as though it were a new prospect.

Likewise, on a return visit, when you previously got an agreement from a prospect as to a need, begin your presentation with something like this:

"As you may recall from my last visit, you said. . . ." Then restate the essence of the agreement and end with, "Isn't that right?"

Here is how Tim Wall might have begun the dialog on his return visit with the dairy farmer.

"As you may recall from my last visit, you said it was important for you to figure out a way to cut down on some of your chores and still produce the same amount of milk. Isn't that right?"

A Misuse of Paraphrasing

There is no good reason to paraphrase facts. Consider this pointless dialog Tim Wall might have had with the dairy farmer:

Tim:	"When was that silo built?"
Farmer:	"1943."
Tim:	"So it's about 40 years old, isn't that right?"
Farmer:	"About that."
Tim:	"How many cows are you milking?"
Farmer:	"Forty-eight."
Tim:	"Close to half a hundred, huh?"
Farmer:	"Pretty close."
Tim:	"Do you have any help on this operation?"
Farmer:	"No."
Tim:	"I gather, then, that you work it all by yourself, right?"
Farmer:	"You got it right."

That kind of conversation is likely to cause irritation. The rule is *paraphrase needs, not facts*.

Here is a recap of what usually takes place in a sales opener using a paraphrase:

1. Give your opening statement.
2. Prospect responds with indifference.
3. Probe for a need. Listen carefully for unexpressed meanings and feelings.
4. Prospect makes a vague statement that hints at or attempts to cover up a need.
5. Paraphrase the prospect's vague statement by rephrasing it into a more specific expression which clarifies the need. Use lead-in phrases such as:

   "What I hear you saying is . . ."
   "I take it, though, that . . ."
   "It sounds as if . . ."
   "As I understand it, you mean . . ."
   "Would it be correct to say . . ."
   "It seems to me . . ."

6. An agreement of the need by the prospect is an important conclusion to a paraphrase. To elicit the agreement, end a paraphrase with a closed-end questioning phrase such as:

   ". . . is that what you mean?"
   ". . . wouldn't it?"

"... isn't it?"
"... that's what you really want, isn't it?"
"... aren't you?"
"... isn't that right?"
"... right?"
"... wouldn't you say?"

When these questions are answered affirmatively, an agreement is being confirmed. It is unlikely that anyone would retract that kind of agreement once it is confirmed.

7. Suggest a benefit your product or service offers that will· satisfy the need.
8. Suggest a time for an appointment to make a complete presentation.

Another Example of Paraphrasing

A retail specialty store has been buying stock direct from various manufacturers because the discount given on direct purchases was substantially more than buying through a wholesale distributor. Another reason carried some emotional overtones. The one time, some years ago, when the owner tried a distributor, he was loaded down with a lot of slow-moving merchandise that eventually had to be sold way below cost. Ever since, he's had no time for distributor reps—that is, until this conversation took place on the telephone.

Brown: Mr. Green, this is Dick Brown of Service Distributing Company.
Green: Hold it. Sorry but I don't buy from distributors. I don't think we have anything to talk about.
Brown: I'm aware that you buy direct, Mr. Green, but while I have you on the phone, do you mind telling me something?
Green: What is it you want to know?
Brown: What do you do with slow-moving merchandise that's been on the shelf for a long time?
Green: It doesn't happen. I order only what I know will sell.
Brown: What about items that customers return for refund?
Green: Well, if it's defective, I pack it and send it back to the manufacturer for credit.
Brown: I'd guess you place orders to each manufacturer by mail or phone as stock needs replenishing, right?

Green: Yes.

Brown: Mr. Green, how do you presently keep track of your inventory?

Green: Well, I take a complete inventory once a year, a modified inventory once a month, and of course I keep an eye on the shelves every day.

Brown: Doesn't all this take up a lot of your time and your employees' time? I mean the ordering, the packing, unpacking individual shipments to and from different sources, taking inventory and all.

Green: Not actually. Been doing it for years. We're still in business. So I guess it's working OK.

Brown: Do you ever miss a sale because you don't have an item a customer wants?

Green: Uh, well, sure, once in a while I suppose. Doesn't everybody?

Something in the way Mr. Green answered this last question made Dick Brown suspect that "once in a while" was more of a concern than Mr. Green was letting on and that it was probably costing him more than a fair amount in customer retention and profitable sales. This can be construed as an indirect expression of a need and a cue for the following paraphrase to bring it out into the open and get Mr. Green to agree to explore the possibility of doing something about it.

Brown: Mr. Green, I take it, though, that if you'd have a more complete stock of merchandise so as to cash in on those missed sales, and if you could order daily from one source on a free WATS line and had daily delivery, guaranteed return for full credit of anything unsalable, one-source billing, plus a monthly printout of your inventory with a forecast of future customer trends—all this requiring no work by you or your staff, you'd sure want to know more about it, wouldn't you?

Green: Well, yes, I suppose so.

That last statement by Mr. Green, the answer to the paraphrase question, is the agreement. It's a turning point in Mr. Green's relationship with distributor salespeople. At last he is admitting he wants to know more about optional ways of operating his business. Now it is natural for Brown to follow this agreement with a summary of benefits and then ask for an appointment to present the full story.

Brown: Mr. Green, our experience with other stores similar to yours shows that they are making many additional sales from special items we stock for them with our computerized inventory control system. This system assures that you will have on hand all the merchandise your customers are likely to ask for, and yet not be overstocked with items that don't sell. Our computer will help you keep an ongoing record of your inventory and make sure it maintains the best balance for your customers' buying patterns. If an item becomes obsolete, we pick it up and you get credit for it at the current price. The result of this is an inventory customized for maximum profit for your store, completely free of obsolescent, slow-moving, or overstocked merchandise. All this is with no* effort on the part of you or your staff. There are many more advantages that you can evaluate in terms of profit to your business, I'd be happy to show you. Can we get together tomorrow morning at 9 or would 1:00 P.M. be better?

A Situation Familiar to Many Salespeople

The fact that this example has to do with a distributor/retailer relationship is not particularly important. A person like Mr. Green is common in many different kinds of business. He may possess any combination of these characteristics: conservative, skeptical, working harder than necessary, bound to tradition, creature of habit, basing important decisions on an isolated past experience, slow to change but having a dimly perceived yet growing realization that things are changing in the business and maybe some of these changes deserve a closer look.

These people need help. They need vendor sales reps who apply initiative, persistence, and skill in their use of questions to probe for needs.

Fine-Tuning Your Approach

Notice in the above example how most of the probing sequence had to do with the prospect's world, not the sales rep's. It also contained a good mix of open- and closed-end questions. As long as Mr. Green was answering questions, it was OK to continue questioning until an important need was uncovered. Notice, too, that the first open-end question concerned a suspected key need and that sustained Mr. Green's interest enough to allow the questioning to continue.

The sales rep didn't uncover Green's strong feelings about the discount differential or the merchandise overload experience. Nor was it necessary to do so in this contact. His objective was to get an appointment to present the full story with Green's mind open. Any objections coming out of those feelings would be better dealt with in person.

Get the Jump on Cherry Pickers

Other distributor reps calling on Mr. Green were cherry pickers who turned tail at his habitual, initial rebuff, which was grounded in a single experience with a short-sighted distributor of another era.

But the nature and scope of distributor operations is changing. They now provide more sophisticated services. Computers enter the picture. Distributors can afford to purchase them and offer retailers benefits that more than pay for the difference in discount.

Look at the changes in your business. Look for innovations that provide unique benefits for your clientele. Look for tradition-bound prospects who need to be brought up to date, especially those who are quick to discourage your opening remarks. It's a safe bet they are doing that to other salespeople who just as quickly turn away looking for someone more congenial. There is less competition for the time and business of skeptics, which make them excellent prospects.

A Case Involving Price Resistance

A perennial objection salespeople must deal with is price resistance. But quality costs more. Quality is usually worth the added cost and it takes skilled and determined salespeople to bring the proof to a resisting marketplace.

A salt company manufactures a high-quality salt. When used in processing meat, it markedly improves the flavor and retards spoilage as compared with ordinary salt. Even though this salt costs more, the benefits of improved salability of meat products due to better taste and longer-lasting freshness make it more than worth the added cost.

Salt sales rep Pat Black makes an opener to Herman Schmaltz, owner of Schmaltz Meat Company. Schmaltz knows of the salt company Black represents. He also knows that its prices are higher than what he is currently paying so he responds to Black's opener by muttering, "I'm not interested in buying your high-priced salt." Black continues by probing:

Black: Mr. Schmaltz, have you read the article in this month's Meat Packing Journal regarding the trend away from chemical preservatives in processing meat?

Schmaltz: It seems to me I remember something like that.

Black: What did you think of it?

Schmaltz: I'm afraid the end result is consumers are going to be disappointed when they find their meat won't last as long in the refrigerator.

Black: Did you also read the article about our HQ salt in that same issue?

Schmaltz: I just glanced through it. But I know one thing. You don't need any kind of fancy salt to cure meat. Good old-fashioned rock salt does just as good and it costs a lot less.

Black: It seems to me, though, that if you could establish consumer preference for a brand that stays fresh longer and tastes better, the increased sales that would result would be well worth putting out a better quality product, wouldn't it?

Schmaltz: It might.

Opening a Closed Mind—An Important First Step

Sometimes the prospect's response to a paraphrase is not total agreement. But even, as in this case, "It might" suggests that he would at least be agreeable to hear more about it. So Black continues:

Black: Mr. Schmaltz, I can show you some interesting case studies of how other meat packers have increased market share with bacon, sausage, ham, and luncheon meats. The studies show how a consumer panel identified their brands as the ones that not only tasted better but gave them longer storage time as well. Would you have twenty minutes to take a look now?

Real Estate for Sale by Owner

A real estate agent knocks on the door of a home with a sign on the lawn, "For Sale by Owner."

Agent: Are you the owner of this house?

Owner: Yes.

Agent: My name is Beth Jones. I'm a realtor. Do you permit realtors to participate in the sale of your house?

Owner: No.

Agent: Have you talked with other realtors?

Owner: Yes, and I told them what I'm going to tell you. We've decided to try and sell it ourselves. We prefer not to pay the commission.

Agent: I can't blame you for wanting to make as much as you can. How long have you had your house for sale?

Owner: About two months.

Agent: Do you have any idea why it hasn't sold yet?

Owner: I guess houses just aren't moving very fast today.

Agent: How did you happen to arrive at your price?

Owner: We just figured this is about what we'd like to get out of it.

Agent: Have you looked at any competitive market data?

Owner: Well, uh, no.

Agent: Don't you think that might be some important information to have?

Owner: I guess we don't know much about that.

Agent: It sounds as if it could be of help to you if we sat down for a few minutes and discussed this. I'd be happy to share some ideas with you about competitive market data, how prices are determined, and how you can arrange some creative financing that could help you close a sale with someone who would like to buy your house but may have some difficulty arranging financing through ordinary channels. Could we do that now?

What to Do When the Need Is Stated

Les Haley sells dishwashing soap to the restaurant trade. He is on the phone to arrange an appointment with G.C. King, a hard-to-see purchasing agent for a large restaurant chain. Les made the mistake of not leading with a benefit, and was almost rebuffed, but wisely did some probing to recover:

Haley: Mr. King, my name is Les Haley with Dynamo Products. Did you have a chance to read the letter I sent you regarding our new low-temp dishwashing detergent?

King: No, I guess I didn't. Dishwashing soap isn't high on my list of concerns. We did a comprehensive value analysis on soap so we're sure we're getting the best product for our money.

Haley Tell me this, Mr. King, where does the cost of energy rate on your list of concerns?

King: That rates pretty high. Actually my biggest concern today is cutting costs. Energy costs for one are getting out of hand. Now if you had something in competition with the gas or electric company, I'd be willing to listen. But soap, no. We're getting the best bang for our buck with soap.

Haley: Actually, Mr. King, the purpose of my call is to arrange an appointment with you when I can show how our low-temperature dishwashing program can appreciably lower your energy costs. For our customers with restaurants averaging $50,000 in food sales per month, our low-temp-program average energy saving is between $1500.00 and $1800.00 per year. I'd be happy to show you how it works. I have some open spots on my schedule Thursday. Would morning or afternoon be better for you?

In this example the prospect brought the need out into the open himself. There is no reason to use a paraphrase here. The prospect is looking for a solution to a problem he is well aware of. So all Les Haley had to do was to state a benefit that offered a solution to the problem and ask for an appointment.

How to Become Expert in Use of the Paraphrase

The technique of paraphrasing is so valuable you will benefit much from reading this chapter several times until you can effortlessly proceed with a paraphrase whenever you hear hints of needs or coverups. As you reread this chapter, recall the times prospects rebuffed your opening remarks and you had good reason to believe they had needs you could satisfy. Perhaps they were only vaguely aware or even totally unaware of their needs.

If possible discuss these situations with other salespeople in your business. Do some creative brainstorming. Practice role-playing these situations with each other. Record these role-play sessions on a tape recorder and critique the playback.

Above all, in the real world of selling, be alert to use paraphrases when you hear vague generalities that hint of possible needs or you hear outright coverups.

An important key to applying tactful and effective persistence that will help you get business that many other salespeople miss is to understand this dimension: People buy because of their needs, wants, problems, and dissatisfactions. Often they are not aware of their needs. Sometimes when they do perceive a need, they are still reluctant to take action. It is an important task of the sales profession to bring these needs into perspective, to guide clientele along a path of making intelligent decisions that will benefit them.

Paraphrasing is a preeminent technique to help you do just that.

17

More on Resistance

Wrong Questions Don't Get Good Answers

How do you handle the prospect who says, "I'm not spending any money"? How do you overcome the skeptic? These are questions I often get from people in my seminar audiences. We are so answer-oriented in our society. In school, there was an answer in the back of the book. There was one right answer to every question. The smart kids and the teacher knew it. It was important to find it out before the test.

But life is not like that. There is usually a lot more to the typical real-life questions than an answer in the back of the book. This is especially true when it comes to dealing with resistance in selling.

To begin with, I take issue with the questions. Consider phrases such as "handle the prospect" and "overcome the skeptic." The words *handle* and *overcome* have a hostile sound. Put yourself in the prospect's place. How do you feel when a salesperson trying to sell you something *handles* or *overcomes* you?

Set the Right Emotional Climate

Of course we must respond to objections with words. And the choice of words is important. By all means select them with considerable deliberation. Write them down. Learn to use them. Memorize them. But those carefully selected words will not work the way you expect if the climate you set is not right, if your attitude is one of an opponent who is trying to handle, overcome, control.

Prospects make decisions to set appointments with salespeople when their emotional reaction to an opener is favorable. They use the logic found in the words to justify their decision after it is made. You get a favorable emotional reaction when prospects perceive you as a knowledgeable professional in some area of their interest who is not a threat to budget, time, or ego. That perception is largely influenced by nonverbal messages.

I've gone to great lengths in covering the knowledgeable professional aspect in this book. Let's now consider the threat aspect of opening climate.

What About the Prospect's Fears?

Much has been said about a salesperson's fear during an opening situation, but think about the prospect. The fear of being sold acts as negatively on prospects as the fear of rejection acts on salespeople. Their ego will not allow them to admit to you that they fear that the boss, or friends, or peers will criticize or ridicule them for making a mistake. Nor would they want to admit to a fear of loss, fear of failure, fear of change. So what do they do? They make a negative remark that is a defensive tactic. They will say, "I'm satisfied with my present situation," or "I'm not interested," or "I'm too busy"— anything to get rid of the feeling of fear, which is very uncomfortable. Logic has nothing to do with this. What you are hearing in the so-called objections are smokescreens. Their purpose is to cloud up the emotional state.

You can answer those smokescreens backward and forward with the most carefully prepared pat answer in the world and you still won't get in the door on the right basis. Because what you are hearing is not the real issue. Your logic does not address the real issue, which is fear.

So what you must do is dissolve the fear or, better yet, take measures to prevent it from cropping up in the first place. You do that by just being yourself. You do it with honesty, patience, understanding, tact, friendliness, a sincere desire to be of service, and without seeing prospects as an enemy or as having your commission dollars in their checking account.

What Goes on Inside of You?

Now back to your own emotional response. If your natural reaction is to flinch when a prospect utters a negative-sounding remark, you're reacting automatically, like Pavlov's dogs who expected food every time a bell rang. We still have a lot of prehistoric-era programming in our bodies. Nature provided us with an extra shot of adrenaline, an extra spurt of energy so we'd be ready to fight the saber-toothed tigers or run away from them.

Resistance in selling is not a life or death matter. We don't need all that much adrenaline pumping. We don't need that much energy. When we allow that to happen, we get defensive (fight); we try to prove we're right with argument. Or we cop out (flight). Either way, nobody wins.

Arguments are primarily logical. You can win them and still lose a chance to make a sale.

The cop-out is often totally nonverbal. It isn't that a salesperson physically runs away. It's just that the conviction is gone from the way the words are delivered.

A Case of Cop-out

Ziggy Loozer is in a slump. He's way behind in his draw and just this morning for the first six calls he heard "not spending a cent," "my budget is overspent," "can't afford it," "we're cutting back," "no way," and "call back in six months." The positive stereo track in his head is disconnected. The negative one is using bad grammar— triple negatives, "nobody ain't buying nothing!" And it's blasting loud and clear.

Ziggy's next call is on Joe Crying, Manager of Crying Towel and Linen Supply Company. Ziggy figured it would help if he could do a better job of establishing rapport with his prospects first. He remembered the sales seminar last week when he learned it was a good idea to ask questions. So he thought he'd try a different opening line.

"Good morning, Mr. Crying. How's business?"

"Terrible," Crying replied, "worst it's ever been. Besides, collections are slow. We've had to lay off one-third of our employees and cut back all spending. Now what is it you want to see me about?"

Ziggy has some good answers to this one because he sells advertising. "Now is the time you really need advertising. It pays! It will boost the morale of your sales force. It will get you more business. It's an investment that will return a profit."

But Ziggy's negative stereo track is still playing. "Yeah, but Crying ain't got no money to spend." And when Ziggy gives out with his carefully prepared phrases, Crying doesn't believe that Ziggy has a solution to his problem for the simple reason that he can tell from the tone of his voice that Ziggy doesn't believe it either. Ziggy copped out!

Interpret with Care

Often a prospect's response to an opener is taken to be an objection by a salesperson when it is not. Take statements such as, "I am very busy," or "I am satisfied with my present source of supply." What do they mean? Are they objections?

A prospect may say, "I am very busy," but he may be thinking, "This sounds like something we could use. I better try to fit it into my schedule," or "I am satisfied with my present source of supply. But maybe there is something better. I'm willing to take a look."

Use a Neutral Response

Because the prospect's response to your opener may be a smokescreen or it may not really be an indication of indifference, or skepticism, or an objection, don't feel compelled to jump in and start answering it. Acknowledge the fact that you heard what was said. But do this with a noncommittal remark such as:

I understand.
I'm not sure I understand.
Oh!

Really.
Hmm.
Is that so?
I see.
That's possible.
That's OK.
That's fine.

These are all neutral comments. "I understand," is neither agreement nor disagreement. "That's OK" and "That's fine" mean that it's OK or fine with you that the prospect said what was said. It's important you stay neutral with your body language also. In other words don't raise your eyebrows or otherwise suggest you doubt, disagree, challenge, or imply any kind of judgment on what the prospect said.

After the neutral comment, ask for clarification if you're not sure what the prospect meant, or continue probing for a need, or if a need is revealed expand or restate your benefit and suggest a time for an appointment.

Suppose a prospect said, "I don't believe I'd be interested."

Don't be too quick to take that at face value. And don't be too quick with a blunt question such as, "But you would be interested in making a profit, wouldn't you?"

Ask Why Tactfully

Even asking "Why do you say that?" can be too blunt. You want an open-end question to get the prospect to open up and tell more about where his or her interests lie. Try this form of *why:* "Obviously, you have a good reason for saying that. Do you mind telling me what it is?"

If you suspect the answer to that question may be a smokescreen, follow up with, "In addition to that, are there any other reasons why you feel you wouldn't be interested?" If the answer is yes, ask, "Would you mind telling me about it?" If the prospect says there are no other reasons, then you have only one reason to deal with. This avoids the ping-pong game in which objections keep coming up and you keep countering with answers. In fact, there is implied agreement that if that one reason were satisfied, you have a green light to proceed.

Welcome Busy Prospects

Obviously, it would not be good judgment to go through this kind of questioning when you have good reason to believe the prospect is busy at an urgent task. Bear in mind, however, that busyness is one of the most common smokescreens heard during an opener. No one sits around just waiting for you to come selling. They're always busy doing something. You come along and interrupt the activity. They want to get back to it. So they say the first thing that comes to mind and that's "I'm busy." Usually something in the way it is said is a tipoff as to how busy they really are. Listen for that!

So when you hear "I'm busy," don't be too quick to withdraw. If you have a person who is in the habit of saying "I'm busy" to most salespeople, you may have an excellent prospect. The competition for his or her time and budget is not as heavy as with other prospects, since few salespeople hang in there. As a matter of fact, when prospects tell you they don't have time to talk to you, and it is true, they are expressing a need to reduce their workload. If one of the benefits of your products is convenience or time saving, you may not need to do any further probing. If that benefit doesn't ring a bell, you probably have a smokescreen. When the busyness is real, suggest rather than ask for another time.

How to Deal with Procrastination

Another common resistance at an opener is procrastination, the tendency to put off making an appointment until some indefinite time in the future. It is important, here, to know what is going on. In the first place, procrastination is an almost universal human trait. Lamentably few live by the dictum "Do it now!" Most will give any excuse as long as it serves to delay a decision.

Secondly, procrastination indicates your opener is only partly effective. You stated a benefit that sounds like something that could satisfy a genuine need. They don't want to close the door on it. They honestly feel they will hear you out at some future date. Yet somehow it just doesn't seem to be an urgent thing to do now.

Come back again at a later date and you can be virtually certain that whatever interest was stirred up the first time will be gone. You're not even back to square one. You're in a minus position. There's a chance your second contact is made at a less convenient time. Keep coming back often enough, you become a pest.

So don't be too quick to settle for a raincheck. It's no points in your favor to be labeled pushy. Yet I rarely ever see sales lost because of too much persistence. But I've seen many opportunities to make sales lost for lack of it. It is so easy for most people to procrastinate when they are faced with the decision of whether to talk to this salesperson further now, or not. They will put you off if you give them the slightest encouragement to do so unless they urgently need what you are selling. You are there. Use good judgment in making the most of it. Be sure that every reason you give to hear you out now is for their benefit, not yours. Keep thinking *when* they will hear your presentation, instead of *whether*. Keep suggesting specific dates. Do it right now. Offer to come right over if you're on the phone.

You won't get through to every procrastinator, but when you know they need what you sell, you are doing them a disservice when you are too quick to retreat. Be thankful there is such a trait as procrastination. If everything were sold because buyers took the initiative to always phone their orders or send them in the mail, there would be no need for salespeople, only order takers. Come to think of it, there would be no need for this book. I'm certainly thankful for procrastinators. They make me feel useful.

Then There Is the Skeptic

Skepticism is another resistance that is sure to be present to some degree in virtually every initial sales contact. It would be a rare person who is completely trusting of strangers, especially those who sell.

Yes, especially those who sell! It goes back to ancient Rome when the code was *caveat emptor,* which means, "let the buyer beware." That code persists today in the minds of most buyers. A popular misconception today is that all salespeople exaggerate, and their ability to do it convincingly is a measure of their sales skill. That misconception is nourished by artless salespeople who lavish their statements with meaningless generalities such as "we're the best," "the greatest," "the number one," "you can't beat this deal," etc. Of course, such banalities are not convincing, but that's part of the misconception.

Because exaggeration is so prevalent, all salespeople must live with the burden that some of their legitimate claims will fall upon skeptical ears. Therefore, the first step to minimizing skepticism is one of prevention. It is important to be aware of the need to build a foundation of believability, nonverbally and verbally, from the very first moment of contact. That is why such things as relaxed manner and eye contact are so vital for in-person calls, likewise voice quality and speed on the phone. You must first deal with skepticism at the emotional level before logic will have any bearing.

Then make sure that what you say is believable and can be backed by proof. But don't come on too quick and too strong with your proof. Making prospects feel sheepish because they were wrong to show skepticism won't help your cause. Then you're back in the wrong emotional zone. Logic won't mean a thing! A time-tested technique for neutralizing skepticism is the familiar "feel, felt, found" formula. It goes like this:

> Mr. Jefferson, I know how you *feel*. Many of our customers have *felt* the same as you do now, when we first approached them with this idea. But they *found*, after using our system, their costs went down considerably, sometimes as much as 30 percent. For example, here is a letter we got from one of our customers, Mr. William Harrison. . . .

This is the classic model of the feel, felt, found formula. I give it here because the words *feel, felt, found* make it easy to remember. Since many salespeople have been trained to use it, I suggest changing the words when calling on experienced professional buyers, to give it a different sound. For example:

It doesn't come as a surprise to hear you say that, Mr. Jefferson. Many of our best customers said the same thing when we first approached them with this idea. Now they've been using our system for years and have realized a substantial cost reduction, in some cases as much as 30 percent. For example, here is a letter we got from one of our customers, Mr. William Harrison. . . .

Then come back with relating the benefit specifically to his situation and close for an appointment.

Taking on the Competition

Another form of indifference comes from the prospect who is buying from one of your competitors and everything is satisfactory. Try this series of questions:

Mr. Prospect, as long as I'm here [or have you on the phone], would you mind if I get your answer to a few questions?
What are the things you like most about doing business with your present supplier?
Why are those things important to you?
What is it you like the least?

You may have some additional questions depending on what is said in response. Be careful you don't directly knock the competition. Keep your ears open for any hint of a need, any possibility that you could do something better in the area of preference or help them to avoid any dissatisfaction. Then summarize with something like this:

Mr. Prospect, just supposing we could provide all the things that are important to you and we could help you avoid the things you don't like, and we could [add an additional benefit or inducement], you would want to know more about it, wouldn't you?

You won't get a yes answer to that last question in 100 percent of the cases. But going through this kind of questioning process will get you a lot more business than retreating from "I'm satisfied with my present supplier." Besides, prospects will know where to find a real pro whenever they need another source of supply.

Boyan's Best Bid

And now for my all-time favorite appointment clincher. Over the years this one got me through countless doors that were almost shut by skepticism or procrastination. It goes like this:

> Mr. Prospect, I wouldn't begin to tell you that you need what I have. That is for you to decide. But I guarantee, you will get enough profitable ideas from our interview to make it well worth your investment of just 30 minutes. Can we do that now, or would tomorrow morning at 8:00 be better?

If there is any chance of a need, if there is the least spark of interest, it is difficult for a reasonable person to turn you away with that offer.

Here is a roundup of ideas that will help you persist when they resist:

1. *Be prepared for resistance.* Don't let it take you by surprise. In the planning stage, mentally rehearse what you will do when a prospect gives you any of the various typical resistances. After a while you won't need to rehearse anymore. Your responses will become second nature.

2. *Relax.* When you hear what sounds like it could be indifference, skepticism, procrastination, smokescreens, or objections, don't be too quick to answer. Your first response should be to relax. Hang loose! Cool it! Make that a conditioned reflex.

3. *Listen.* Hear them out. Listen with a sincere desire to understand their point of view. Avoid any hint with body language or vocally that you are eager to step on their lines and start giving your answer or that you imply any judgment to what you hear. You may be champing at the bit to answer, but don't do it. Listen for the feelings behind their words. They will give you the best clues how to proceed.

4. *Paraphrase.* When you hear vague generalities or suspect a coverup of a need, restate the prospect's words in more concrete language. End the paraphrase in the form of a question that seeks agreement to your version of what was meant.

5. *Narrow it down.* If the prospect gives you a definite reason

why you are not being granted an interview, find out if it's the only one.

6. *Question it*. Use a tactful form of asking why. Continue probing for a need.

7. *State a benefit that relates to a need*.

8. *Suggest a time for an appointment*. Always be thinking *when* not *if* the prospect will grant you an interview. Don't hesitate at the conclusion of your benefit statement. Take the initiative to suggest a time. Don't ask the prospect when it would be convenient. You suggest alternative times. The sooner the better.

All things considered, the nonverbal aspect of dealing with resistance far outweights the importance of the words you choose. But remember, it's the attitude you bring into the relationship that forms your nonverbal response. And that attitude is a choice you make.

Many unpredictable things happen in sales relationships. One thing that is absolutely predictable is you will meet with resistance. It's the very reason for the existence of the sales profession. Be thankful for it. Let its challenge be a part of your professional growth.

18

Making It Work for You

Adult education is one of the fastest growing industries of the late years of the twentieth century. That sounds like an understatement to those of us in this profession as we see the phenomenal growth bursting forth.

Billions of dollars are spent every year on a profusion of books and manuals; audio, video, and computer-based programs; seminars and consultants, all focused on helping people become more effective on their jobs and in living their lives. You could never compute the total investment in these programs, as you would have to factor in the dollars of revenue lost by revenue producers taken off the job to participate in some learning process. That would be impossible to determine.

Corporations are the advance guard of innovation in training adults, and they pick up the biggest share of the tab. Corporations are also on the cutting edge of designing methods of accountability to assure their money is wisely spent. The buzz word in corporate training is *performance*. Top decision makers found out long ago that training efforts are a total waste unless there is a performance payoff in the real world.

One of the best methods that training-wise corporations use to protect their investment is known as the *learning contract*. Those who are granted the privilege of adding to their professional growth at the company expense must commit in writing what they intend to do differently as a result of their training experience.

I suggest you make a learning contract with yourself in order to capitalize on what you learned from this book. If you are in the habit of underlining or otherwise marking the places in a book that were important to you, that's fine. If not, go back over the book and pick out the ideas that could be especially helpful to you. In particular, reread Chapter 3. How will your performance change as a result? Set some new performance goals for yourself. Put them in writing, make them specific and measurable, and date them.

As I mentioned earlier, people resist doing this. Remember my friend who wanted to play the guitar and threw his written goal statement in the waste basket. Most people are like that when it comes to changing routine. It is easier to fall back into old comfortable habits of doing what produces some results—that earn a living, that get by—so why change?

We resist change for a reason that I believe is an illusion. And that is, it just *seems* easier to adapt to whatever inconvenience is brought on from settling for less—less personal satisfaction, less financial reward—than it is to adapt to the inconvenience of doing what is necessary to make a better way of life.

If you would choose to enjoy the rewards of a bigger dimension in life, the joy of a greater use of the potential talents and abilities you have, let me suggest an important thing you must do: YOU MUST FORM NEW HABITS. Because, if you keep conducting your affairs in the same way that you have habitually been doing in the past, you can only expect to get the same kind of results. If you want to produce better results, then you must *do* things differently. And this doing must become a habit. If we do not deliberately choose to form productive habits, it is most probable we will unconsciously form habits that are more pleasing but less productive.

Horace Mann gave us this bit of wisdom: "Habit is like a cable. We weave a thread of it every day, and at last we cannot break it."

Good luck and good selling.

References

p. 1. Taken from *Fiddler on the Roof* by Joseph Stein. Copyright © 1964 by Joseph Stein. Used by permission of Crown Publishers, Inc.

p. 6. Viktor Frankl, *Man's Search for Meaning* (New York: Simon & Schuster, 1970).

p. 8. Albert Ellis, "Rational Psychotherapy," in *The Journal of General Psychology*, 1958, 59: 35–49. For a fuller discussion, see Albert Ellis and Robert A. Harper, *A New Guide to Rational Living* (North Hollywood, Cal.: Wilshire Book Co, 1975).

p. 8. Maxwell Maltz, *Psycho-Cybernetics* (West Nyack, N.Y.: Parker Publishing Co, 1960).

p. 16. Jard DeVille, *Nice Guys Finish First* (New York: William Morrow, 1978).

p. 19. Erich Fromm, *The Art of Loving* (New York: Harper & Row, 1956).

p. 20. See Robert Conklin, *The Dynamics of Successful Attitudes* (Englewood Cliffs, N.J.: Prentice-Hall, 1963), for the details of his philosophy. Conklin's earlier book *The Dynamics of Positive Attitudes* is out of print.

p. 23. Lewis Carroll, *Alice in Wonderland,* in Martin Gardner, ed., *The Annotated Alice* (New York: Clarkson N. Potter, 1960), p. 88.

p. 51. Harry Overstreet, *The Mature Mind* (New York: W. W. Norton, 1949).

p. 73. *The Music Man* by Meredith Willson, © 1957 Frank Music Corp. and Rinimer Corporation. Song "Ya Got Trouble" © 1958, 1966.

p. 156. Edmund Jacobson, *You Must Relax* (New York: McGraw-Hill, 1978).

p. 156. David Harold Fink, *Release from Nervous Tension* (New York: Simon & Schuster, 1962).

p. 156. Herbert Benson and Miriam Z. Klipper, *The Relaxation Response* (New York: Avon, 1976).

Index